A PLUM ASSIGNMENT

A PLUM ASSIGNMENT

DISCOURSES ON P. G. WODEHOUSE AND HIS WORLD

BY

CURTIS ARMSTRONG

AND

ELLIOTT MILSTEIN

Winch and Clutterbuck

"Publishers of the book beautiful"

ISBN 978-0-692-08631-5

Quotations from P. G. Wodehouse are reprinted by permission of The Trustees of the Wodehouse Estate.

Editing, book design, and cover design by Ashley D. Polasek, PhD, FRSA
Front cover image by Nathan Milstein
Photograph of Curtis Armstrong and Elliott Milstein, ca 1976, by Ken Fink

Printed and bound in the United States of America

Published by Winch and Clutterbuck
Bensonburg, Long Island
New York 11701

Across the pale parabola of Joy...

—*Ralston McTodd*

CONTENTS

FOREWORD

This is a book about P. G. Wodehouse. But it is also a book about two friends.

That it was Wodehouse who brought Curtis Armstrong and Elliott Milstein together is no surprise, at least not to me. Pelham Grenville Wodehouse (known to his family and fans as "Plum") has been the catalyst for many an abiding friendship, and even for several weddings. I myself can claim both a best friend and a blissful marriage thanks to Wodehouse. I can also claim a camaraderie with the authors of this book: I've been chums with Elliott since the early 1990s and have known Curtis since 2003. So when I read the tale of their meeting in high school, I could readily appreciate the sunshine that came into their lives then and continues to brighten their lives now.

I assume that most who come to this book are, like me, already pretty familiar with Wodehouse's work and already appreciate that P. G. Wodehouse was a writer's writer, able to string words together in such a way that any literate human being couldn't help but be breathless with admiration—and with laughter. You will enjoy a similar experience in this entertaining book, which will add significantly to your appreciation of Plum's work and world. However, it is just possible that some of you have read most or even all of his books without knowing anything about the context in which Curtis and Elliott's articles were created or the communities of devotees that exist to celebrate Wodehouse.

Of the many associations devoted to Wodehouse that have sprung up around the world, you will hear frequent mention of two of them in particular. One is The P G Wodehouse Society (UK), which was founded in 1997 and, among other activities, holds a formal dinner at Gray's Inn, London, every two years. The dinner highlights are a toast written and delivered by a Very Important Person and a post-prandial entertainment performed by Wodehouse's step-grandchildren and guest celebrities. Elliott and Curtis themselves have, respectively, performed these illustrious roles to acclaim at bygone dinners.

Then there is The Wodehouse Society (aka TWS), founded in Pennsylvania in 1980. That's right—although Wodehouse is better known in the U.K., the Americans were first to establish a long-lasting fan club for Plum; they even named their quarterly journal *Plum Lines*, the journal that originally published many of the pieces you are about to read. Since 1981, TWS has held a biennial, weekend-long convention somewhere in North America, hosted by one of its twenty-seven regional chapters. These chapters adopt their whimsical names from the Wodehouse Canon, such as Elliott's local chapter in Detroit, the Pickering Motor Company, and Curtis's local chapter in Los Angeles, the Perfecto-Zizzbaum Motion Picture Corporation. Convention weekends are filled with fun and activity, the center of which are entertaining and enlightening talks presented by both well-known and not-so-well-known Wodehouseans, some of them scholars, some not.

Two of TWS's most popular convention speakers are—you guessed it—Elliott Milstein and Curtis Armstrong. Elliott's involvement with the Society goes back to its earliest days, and he was its president from 1995 to 1997. He gave his first convention talk at the Kalamazoo, Michigan, gathering in 1989, with six more following in the years since then. Curtis climbed aboard some time later. In addition to reading the talks themselves, you, lucky reader, are about to hear the inside story of how that came to be.

Two other regular convention speakers are worth noting here because their names appear frequently in this book. One is Tony Ring, a founder member of the U.K. Society whose contributions to Wodehouse scholarship would take pages to list. Perhaps his crowning achievement is the outstanding and invaluable *Millennium Wodehouse Concordance*, an eight-volume reference project begun by the late Geoffrey Jaggard.

The other is my late husband, Norman Murphy, the founding Chairman of the U.K. Society. Norman's passion was finding and explaining the real-life origins of Wodehouse's settings, characters, and references. He not only documented all that in his books—in particular *In Search of Blandings* (1981) and *A Wodehouse Handbook* (2006; revised 2013)—he also conducted free Wodehouse Walks in London for more than thirty years, educating and entertaining hundreds of Wodehouse fans from all over the globe, including Elliott and Curtis (along with Curtis's brilliant daughter, Lily).

And now, just as they were once guided by Norman, and as, indeed, they have always been guided by each other, so Elliott and Curtis will guide you through their own insights and their own shared journey as readers, speakers, and friends.

The world of Wodehouse is filled to the brim with joy and laughter, making it no wonder that so many friendships have begun in a shared admiration for this amazing writer. The ties that bind Curtis and Elliott as friends are manifold, of course, but Wodehouse was the first and remains one of the strongest. This is evident in how they describe their relationship and introduce each other's papers: with humor, affection, admiration, and boundless respect. Wodehouse, had he known them, would have likened them to Damon and Pythias.

So sit back and prepare to enjoy a book that will inform and entertain you about both P. G. Wodehouse and two dashed wonderful friends—who, by the way, are no slouches in the writing department themselves.

Elin Woodger Murphy
London, England
January 2018

From the Desk of Curtis Armstrong
Los Angeles, CA
16 July, 2017

Who Is This Remarkable Boy?

There is a curious freemasonry among the bookishly inclined. Take two people from different backgrounds and upbringing, different religions, different politics. These are people who on the surface would appear to have a limited shelf life when it comes to friendship. There would be, perhaps, just too many hurdles, too many limitations of shared interests to make a long-term relationship possible. It might seem, just possibly, a little too much like work.

But bibliophiles are of a different breed. They can be dissimilar in a wide range of ways—even antithetical in basic philosophies and beliefs—and can still be brought into the tightest of bonds by an object a mere 8" by 5" in size, consisting of a few hundred delicate sheets of paper with letters printed all over them, bound together on one side with glue, and sometimes with a picture slapped on the front.

Paperback books were initially just a cheap way for publishing houses to make money and, once the copyright act was passed, for authors to get enough royalty payments thrown their way to keep them in tobacco, cocktails, and golf balls. They weren't really intended to last. If a paperback book published in the fifties or early sixties was still holding together and readable by the early seventies, it was because someone took care of it.

Elliott Milstein and I loved books, and we took care of them. It turns out, that's why we became friends. We took care of our Wodehouse books, and it was our Wodehouse books that brought us together.

Our recollections of our first meeting differ. We were both members of Berkley High School's Technical Theatre Workshop: We are agreed on that. But my memory of this encounter has a little less of the Stanley and Livingstone significance to it than his does. In fact, as I recall, it wasn't even Wodehouse that brought us together, initially, but Ian Fleming. I was carrying one of my cherished James Bond novels (It was *Dr. No*, a copy printed in paperback by Pan in 1966, blue cover with a black spider-web design. It is still on my bookshelves and I re-read that very copy just three years ago.) Elliott, whose father owned many books published in paperback by English publishing houses like Pan and Penguin, recognized the distinctive Pan logo on the spine of the book and asked in astonishment where I had gotten it, for Pan books were unavailable in the U.S. They were certainly never seen carried around by high school students.

I told him I'd purchased it while living overseas. (I'd spent several years in Switzerland, and Fleming—along with P. G. Wodehouse—was among the most popular authors at the English Bookstore in Geneva.) As far as I recall, that was as far as the conversation went. Maybe we exchanged a reflective look when we parted, as if to say, "Who is this remarkable boy, with his easy familiarity with foreign imprints? He may be worth cultivating...."

The discovery of our mutual love of Wodehouse was yet aborning. When it did happen, the effect was seismic. Elliott, when relating this event over the years, gets it essentially right, except it took a while to realize we shared other nerdy affinities, such as a love of tea, chess, and Baroque music, though I must say I never cared for Vivaldi. Aside from that, though, spot on, old man.

My Wodehouse journey had begun in Geneva when an English friend lent me his copy of *Very Good, Jeeves* with a strict injunction to return it when I was finished with it. It was one of the volumes that those of us of a certain vintage remember fondly: a cream and orange cover with a non-canonical cover illustration by Geoffrey Salter of Bertie in faultless evening dress, looking fraught, hanging by rings over the swimming bath at the Drones Club, while Jeeves stands off to the side holding a towel. That copy was printed in 1962. In the back of the book is a list of what is delightfully described as "Other Humorous Penguins Available for Purchase." It includes a number of Wodehouse titles as well as several "Doctor" books by Henry Cecil. One of Cecil's titles, called *Friends at Court*, is accompanied by a blurb from Wodehouse himself: "Cecil better than ever!" (The admirable brevity of the encomium has always suggested to me that Wodehouse hadn't actually read the book, but dashed off this faint praise as a favor to his publisher.) This edition of *Very Good, Jeeves*, by the way, was priced at three shillings and sixpence, which even in 1962 was a deal. It turned out I didn't even have to pay that much for it since I never returned it to my friend, which made it even a better deal, especially when you consider this unexceptional-looking little book quite literally changed my life.

Book folk know the feeling well. That moment, often mere seconds after opening the cover of a book, when one realizes that light will be shining a little more brightly from now on. It happened to me exactly two other times: on first reading Conan Doyle and Washington Irving. In all three cases, the feeling is the same: that slightly breathless sense that you have just met one of your Great Loves. It's a feeling we don't often experience even when meeting one of our actual, flesh and blood Great Loves. When you're eleven, or whatever age I was when I first read *Very Good, Jeeves*, you haven't had that experience anyway. You just know that in some indefinable and mysterious way, you've fallen and fallen hard. The first story in this book was called "Jeeves and the Impending Doom," and this was the first paragraph I read:

> It was the morning of the day on which I was slated to pop down to my Aunt Agatha's place at Woolam Chersey in the county of Herts for a visit of three solid weeks; and as I seated myself at the breakfast table, I don't mind confessing that the heart was singularly heavy. We Woosters are men of iron, but beneath my intrepid exterior at that moment there lurked a nameless dread.

This is not the place for me to do an analysis of just how brilliant those two sentences are, but I defy any lover of books with even a shred of a sense of humor to go that far in this book and no farther. I was a well-read boy, but this…the subtleties! Just the fact that he didn't say "my heart," but "THE heart"! It was funny, but why? And where the hell was "Woolam Chersey"? Or "Herts," for that matter? I had never encountered either before, and it didn't matter. I had the strange sensation that I was reading a book written in an alien tongue, but someone had implanted a chip in my cerebral cortex so that I could understand every word, get every inside joke. Sorcery, I call it.

When I met Elliott Milstein, to put it in English-Public-School terms, I was at Wooster House and he was a Blandings boy. In time, we coaxed each other into our favorite sagas, and we discovered everything thereafter together, from the highs of *Leave it to Psmith* to the depths of *Doctor Sally*. We may have howled with laughter reading works of undisputed genius like *Summer Lightning* out loud, but we also had in one another a sympathetic scholar who would listen as the other was struggling his way through less inspired stuff like *If I Were You*. We could be disputatious, too, arguing and debating the merits of *Uneasy Money* or the reason for something like *The Coming of Bill* even existing. (Elliott's theory that it was Wodehouse attempting to write in the style of D. H. Lawrence was palpable nonsense. He just hated *The Coming of Bill* so much that he came up with that explanation because if there was anything Elliott hated more than *The Coming of Bill*, it was anything by D. H. Lawrence.)

And now here we are, decades later, still as deep into it as ever. Elliott discovered The Wodehouse Society (TWS) first and plunged with a kind of giddy abandon into their light-hearted traditions and celebrations, while I, the professional performer and apparent extrovert for whom this sort of cheerful nonsense would appear to have been invented, stood shyly off to the side. I applauded his eventual election to the presidency of the Society, but even that wasn't enough to draw me in at first. Over time, though, happily, he wore down my resistance. We both wrote papers, lots of them as it turned out, either for publication or for reading at the rambunctious Society meetings, or both. They are all included in this book, and as such stand not just as earnest and whimsical Wodehouse scholarship, but as a series of affectionate snapshots of a lasting friendship based in two book nerds' abiding passion for The Master, P. G. Wodehouse.

From the desk of Elliott Milstein
Detroit, MI
16 July, 2017

We've Been Friends Ever Since

D espite Curtis's attestation, it really was P. G. Wodehouse that brought us together.

Of course, I'd known Curtis Armstrong before Wodehouse came into the picture. We were in the same theatre class at Berkley High School, despite his being a year younger. I was a senior, and he was a junior. Normally, a chasm this wide in high school could not be bridged, but we were both in Technical Theatre Workshop (TTW), one of the three nerd classes that mixed class years (the others being Band and Choir). So we not only knew each other, but actually toiled side by side on various theatrical events.

Whilst Curtis's interest in acting began as soon as his little lips could lisp (try saying *that* five times quickly), my love affair with the theatre began suddenly and overwhelmingly when my father took me to New York during Christmas break of my junior year. I saw three plays, fell head over heels in love, and came home determined to be a playwright.

Before that, I was the classic Nerd. Read exclusively science fiction and fantasy (no Wodehouse yet). Listened only to classical music. Wore a sports jacket and carried a briefcase to school. Oh, I also had a pocket protector. Really. I needed it because I used a fountain pen. Yeah. You get the idea.

But that trip to New York changed me. Soon I was wearing black turtle neck sweaters, smoking a pipe (okay, that was still a little nerdy, but kinda cool, don't you think?), reading existentialism, and starting to write my first play. I also dropped band and calculus my senior year to enroll in Drama Class and TTW, and it was there, as I said, I met Curtis.

Curtis had only rather recently returned from living in Switzerland (for a full description of Curtis's life, I recommend purchasing his memoir, *Revenge of the Nerd (or the singular adventures of the man who would be Booger)*, available from St. Martin's Press, 2017), so he was still pretty much in full nerd mode, while I was trying hard to exit it. A year younger than most of us, shy and retiring by nature, he hung around on the periphery of class, keeping pretty much to himself.

Until he got on stage, that is. Then it was a completely different story.

Berkley High School put on two plays a year: the winter play, put on just before Christmas break, and the spring play, put on just after Easter. That year, our winter play was *Auntie Mame*. I had a small walk-on role in the first scene. Curtis also had a walk-on, but his was in the second act. He had one line. He stole the show. The girl who starred as Auntie Mame never forgave him.

For me, the exciting part of the experience was not so much watching this nerdy kid come alive as a comic genius, but the fact that I had come up with an idea of how to do the scene, so our teacher let me direct it. From that moment on, I wanted to be a director as well. Directing Curtis was sheer joy as his approach to acting, even then, was light years beyond all the other kids. And I had the distinct pleasure of doing it twice more after that, and it only got better as he went from student to professional.

But none of this has anything to do with P. G. Wodehouse. Here's where the Wodehouse motif comes in:

It was the job of the students of TTW to build the sets and do all the technical work for the two shows—lighting, sound, etc. In the first semester, we needed to learn the skills to do this; then, we needed to actually do it for the winter play. But in the second semester, having already mastered the skills, there really wasn't anything for us to do until around March, so for two months, we basically goofed off.

One day when I wasn't roaming the halls or trying to pick up the girls in class, I was sitting in the back of the theatre reading, if memory serves, *Heavy Weather*. The reason I think it was *Heavy Weather* is that I had only just started reading Wodehouse a month or so before, and *Heavy Weather* was the second Wodehouse I had read. I should have been reading Wodehouse for much longer, but there were, shall we say, problems.

Like Curtis, my bibliophilia began quite early—I think when I first read, "Look, Jane. See Spot run." As far back as I can remember, I was never happier than when lying on the couch immersed in a book. I read pretty much anything I could get my hands on, and, with my father's library quite open to me, I got my hands on some pretty interesting stuff. There is quite a famous story in my family about when I was sent to the principal's office in sixth grade because I brought a James Bond book to school (it was *Thunderball*, not that it matters, and, yes, it was the Pan edition) and was caught reading the racy bits to my friends. The principal called my father to let him know of this unacceptable behavior. My father's response is famous in Milstein family lore: "Thank you so much for informing me," he told the principal; "I had no idea his reading was so advanced."

But it did prompt him to take more of an interest in what I was getting into, and, when I complained that I had read everything of interest for kids my age (I had finished off all the Tom Swift, Danny Dunn and Henry Reed books, you understand), he decided to guide me to more wholesome fare than Ian Fleming.

Handing me his tattered old *Nothing but Wodehouse*, he instructed me to begin at the end with *Leave it to Psmith*. Now if this were a fairy tale, I would tell you that from that moment on I never looked back, but I must be totally honest with you. I found it silly. I did not even get through the first chapter, and I returned it to him. He muttered something underneath his breath—I think it was "Youth! Youth!"— and, bending to my science fiction proclivities, sent me off with a Jules Verne, which set me on a new course that kept me busy and out of trouble for some time.

Around the age of fifteen, I underwent another period of ennui, having polished off Verne, Wells, Poe and the like, and returned to him for advice. He slipped *Jeeves in the Offing* into my hand. I made it past the first chapter, but not much farther than that. "This guy's an idiot," I said, handing the book back to him. "But that's the point," he replied. "I don't see much of a point in that," said I, and spent the next two years wallowing in murder mysteries.

By the age of seventeen, I was far too cool to ask my father for advice, so being bored during Christmas break and once again out of ideas for something to read, I began prowling his library. In my mind, I can still see the Wodehouse shelf—it was the second from the top, a series of Penguins about three feet long. I climbed up onto the counter and began to look at the titles. *Service with a Smile* caught my attention as a pleasant title, so I pulled it down. Finally, I get to say it: I never looked back!

Now back to TTW in January, 1971. You remember the scene: I am in the back of the theatre reading *Heavy Weather*. Curtis saw me and was drawn like a moth to flame. He approached warily. Even though we had conversed and worked together, he was still a little afraid to actually accost an upperclassman. But he couldn't help himself.

> "Excuse me," he said, like a timid fawn peering through the undergrowth, "but is that Wodehouse you're reading?"
>
> "Yes," I replied, looking down from lazy eyelids and flicking an invisible speck of dust from my immaculate Mechlin lace cuff.
>
> "Wow, that's incredible. I didn't know anyone else around here read Wodehouse. I've been reading his books for years."
>
> Not wanting to reveal that I was new to the Master, thereby putting myself in an inferior position to this callow youth, I adopted an even more aloof demeanor, like a monarch deigning to cavort with a member of the canaille. "Yes, I frequently like to relax with a good Wodehouse before bedtime while having my evening cup of tea or listening to a little Vivaldi."

Curtis's world rocked. He had no idea that there was anyone on this continent—other than himself—who read Wodehouse, drank tea, and listened to Baroque chamber music, let alone that such a fellow existed in his own school.

Well, to make a long story short, we've been friends ever since. Six months later, I decamped to Toronto, and we never again resided in the same city, but we corresponded faithfully and visited each other at least four or five times a year, although that was often in Detroit when we were visiting our parents. (I mean that he was visiting his parents while I was visiting mine.)

We agreed that after we graduated from college, we would both move to New York and go into the theatre together—he as actor and me as writer-director. Well, he, famously, went on to fulfill his destiny as star of stage, film, and TV, while for me the dream died shortly after college, primarily because, while he was immensely talented, you could fit my talent into a thimble and still have plenty of room for your index finger.

But in all the letters and, later, emails, and in all the late-night conversations over brandy and pipes, books and reading were a constant subject, and Wodehouse, in particular, was always a *leit motif*. We differed somewhat in our approach and appreciation of many things, even in Wodehouse, so there was always plenty to share and discuss. Sometimes, when we were together, we just read aloud. Curtis, of course, did most of the reading, while I just laughed. And I mean *laughed*. One night in particular stands out. We were in Toronto for a long weekend in the summer. Ensconced in a cell-like dorm room and settling in for the night, Curtis began reading a passage from *Summer Lightning*. Soon I was laughing harder and harder, and finally he joined in and could barely get the words out. We both almost passed out from lack of oxygen.

For Curtis, Wodehouse was an interest that stood in the company of many others, such as Conan Doyle, Washington Irving, Dickens, Hardy, and, God forgive him, D. H. Lawrence. For me, Wodehouse was, at least for a decade or so, a singular obsession. Where Curtis dropped in on Wodehouse from time to time—reading and re-reading his favorite dozen or so novels and short stories, while visiting many other residents in that vast city of English literature—I rather moved in with him, as it were, reading everything he wrote and everything written about him. I ultimately did my undergraduate thesis on him, joined The Wodehouse Society (TWS), and pretty much dedicated myself to reading and collecting everything Wodehouse. Our personal libraries are of a comparable size, but Curtis's is much more eclectic. Wodehouse dominates mine. Whilst Curtis has written and been published on many different authors, musicians, and other subjects, my total critical output has been about Wodehouse alone.

It has always been a dream of mine to collect my writings on Wodehouse into one volume and publish it, but modesty forbade. A number of years ago, however, I got the idea of asking Curtis if he would consent to be a co-author and include his sublime works as well, giving the book added appeal and considerably improving the

overall quality (not to mention sheer entertainment value). He gener-
ously agreed, leaving the compilation process entirely to me. I got the
idea of adding interstitial pieces to original works, but Curtis was, by
this time, completely absorbed in finishing his memoirs, and the project languished. Once *Revenge of the Nerd* was completed, however, he
rejoined with a vengeance, recommending a significant change in the
direction and compass of the project. I, of course, agreed unreservedly.
He long ago proved to me his superior sensibilities.

It was the summer of 1983. Curtis called me one night and told
me he was offered this strange part in this weird film called *Revenge of
the Nerds*, and he wasn't sure if he should take it. It wasn't a character
that really appealed to him—a guy who picked his nose for laughs and
was called "Booger." The money was good, though, and a job was a
job after all. I think he was kind of asking my permission to do the
film. Fortunately, I was there to keep him on the right track: "Don't be
ridiculous," I said. "Your comic genius is subtle and wry, not slapstick.
Give it a miss."

Well, as history notes, he ignored my advice, to his benefit and the
enormous benefit of the millions who have enjoyed that performance.
As a result, I have followed his advice ever since. And now you, as the
reader of this book, are poised to benefit from that as much as I have.

From the desk of C.
Los Angeles, CA
2 August, 2017

More Than a Little Sunshine

I remember the early 1990s, when Elliott delivered the following talk, as the period when I, as a Wodehousean, was a solitary wanderer in the wilderness. My involvement in organized Wodehouse fandom at that time was practically non-existent. Once, on a Sunday afternoon, I had gone to the King's Head Pub in Santa Monica to attend an early organizational meeting of what was, years later, to become The Perfecto-Zizzbaum Corporation—the Los Angeles chapter of TWS. I thought it would be an amusing idea if I wore a chrysanthemum in my buttonhole so I would be recognized, as Psmith did on his first meeting with Freddie Threepwood in *Leave it to Psmith*. I was chagrined to discover on my arrival that the three other men present thought as highly of idea as I and were also wearing chrysanthemums in their buttonholes. We looked like a convention of funeral directors.

I had also shyly contributed my first paper—"My Contribution to Wodehouse Scholarship"—to the quarterly journal of TWS, *Plum Lines*. It had prompted the paper's then-editor, the great Ed Ratcliff, to leave a message on my machine asking me to call him at once. He had just received the article, he said, and he must speak with me immediately. Swelling a little with pride, for the man was clearly impressed by my little effort, I called back only to have him tell me, practically in tears with gratitude, how wonderful it was that my paper came in under one page. "People write these papers that go on and on and I have to redo the layout over and over and do jump pages and so on, but this…it's just the perfect size! Thank you!"

So, as I say, my connection with the Wodehouse world was tenuous at best. Not so Elliott. I watched in amazement as he bounded, gazelle-like, up the rocky inclines of The Wodehouse Society. The man not only attended these weekends, but delivered scholarly papers to the gathered scholars to boot. Well, he had done it once at that point in 1989, but here he was in 1991, back at the podium like he'd been doing it for years. I'd been impressed by his first talk when I read it afterward, but this new one really made me sit up and take notice.

I can talk with some confidence about this paper because I know it practically back to front, thanks to the late, deeply lamented Ken Fink. This Fink, a witty and large-hearted restaurateur/journalist who, ten years earlier, had shown up on my doorstep with Milstein and some stale baked goods—a story for which the reader is not yet prepared, but which does in fact appear later in these chaotic memoirs—had filmed the 1991 speeches, and much of the dinner as well, as an historical document. Elliott had sent me a copy of it on a VHS tape, and I watched it probably twenty times.

There were other talks, some of them fine. There were also some extraordinarily drunk people present. Most were still at the expansive, slightly glazed-of-eye stage, while one had reached almost Gussie Fink-Nottlian levels of public inebriation and had to be practically pried off the microphone. At one point, mysteriously, the air in the dining room appeared to be full of bats. On closer examination, they proved to be dinner rolls. This spirited tradition—the throwing of bread in the dining room—was based on one established by the denizens of the fabled Drone's Club but even then was considered controversial. Clearly seen on the film of that dinner is one roll thrown with uncanny accuracy from across the room and down the front décolletage of one attendee's evening gown. This helps to date the dinner: The throwing of bread rolls at Wodehouse dinners was suppressed only a few years later.

Watching that tape gave me a connection to the Wodehouse community that I would not otherwise have enjoyed. And because I've had the foresight to keep my VHS player in good working order, I was able to enjoy it again just the other day.

As entertaining as the whole thing is, it's still Elliott's talk that stands out, and not just because he was my friend, either. This is true scholarship. Elliott alone could take an analysis of the opening paragraphs of Wodehouse's novels and magically deliver up everything from spondee feet in *The Luck of the Bodkins*, to the number of prepositional or independent clauses before reaching subject or predicate in the opening of

Joy in the Morning, or the percentage of Wodehouse's books that begin with an image of sunshine.

Indeed, there is more than a little sunshine in this paper, scattered with a generosity that Uncle Fred himself would appreciate.

A STUDY OF THE OPENINGS
OF THE NOVELS OF P. G. WODEHOUSE

Elliott Milstein

First given as a talk at The Wodehouse Society Convention in New York, NY in 1991 and published in Plum Lines *in Spring 1992. Revised and given again at The Wodehouse Society Convention in Seattle, WA in 2015 with the title "It Wasn't a Dark and Stormy Night" and with the original title as a sub-title. The revised version had a different opening and conclusion, but was substantially the same and never published in that form. It is presented here in its original version.*

Some time ago, and though quite a while after the last convention of this society still flush from, may I say, my success at the gathering in Kalamazoo, I decided to once again compose some little effort on the works of the Master whom we are all here to honor. But even as I reached said decision, I knew that, given the exigencies of my busy life—a fifty hour a week job and two ruthlessly cute children being but two of the demands placed on my time—whatever topic I chose would have to require very little research, a prospect daunting, need I say, when one contemplates the task of reviewing the works of a man whose total life-time output includes seventy novels, some two hundred short stories, and over forty plays and musicals, not to mention extraneous song lyrics, essays, articles, and other morceaux generated in between. I could, of course, choose some minor topic like, say, "The Accuracy of the Characterization of Swans in 'Jeeves and The Impending Doom'" or "Ukridge and the Theory of Supply-Side Economics," either of which would, naturally, make all the research necessary for such a paper but a single evening affair, but would, I fear, be a shade narrow and pedantic, and besides, from the very beginning of my interest in Wodehouse criticism, I have rather eschewed that branch of study which combs an author's works for minutiae of limited interest and have chosen rather to look upon the oeuvre as a whole, trying to divine patterns, developments, and motifs common throughout, so in composing this current effort, I was not about to abandon the habit of a lifetime—a habit, I may add, which bagged me an A+ on my thesis at the University of Toronto, a little effort some of you may know called "The Growth of Sweetness and Light, a study of the novels of P. G. Wodehouse."

It was while attempting to find an answer to this conundrum that I picked up the new Flashman book by George MacDonald Fraser. Eagerly I tore the book open, as I always do with the latest Flashman, for you see, Fraser has this knack of beginning his novels with these great opening sentences. And it was while I was mentally picking apart his latest effort that an electric shock shook the frame, and I leaped a clear six inches into the air, shouting, if I remember correctly, "Eureka," for the answer to my difficulty hit me square in the glabellum: why not analyze Wodehouse's openings? While it might be a tad time-consuming to read the opening sentences of every Wodehouse book, it was certainly a lot less time-consuming than re-reading the entire Canon. And with luck, some interesting pattern might emerge. As it happens, such an effort turned out to be rather illuminating, especially in light of the results of my research fifteen years ago in Toronto.

Those of you "privileged" to have read my ground-breaking thesis will remember that I divided Wodehouse's writing career into three periods, which I quite cleverly called Early, Middle and Late.[1] The Early Period, from 1900 to 1923, is marked first by what the great Wodehouse scholar Richard Usborne calls "the apprenticeship years" using the boys' school stories to learn his craft and, in the second half, what I call his "years of search," breaking into the adult market as he cast about for a style or form or voice, as it were, all his own. I think he found his style in *Leave it to Psmith*. From the completion of this work

---

1   For a more in-depth presentation of this argument, see "The Growth of Sweetness and Light: A Study in the Novels of P. G. Wodehouse," pp. 128-157 of this book.

through the composition of the first third of *Full Moon*, I call the Middle Period. Some call this period his "vintage years" because the plots of the novels he wrote at this time are so complex and his prose so rich and full-bodied. In the twenties and thirties, Wodehouse was clearly writing at the height of his powers. His narrative voice is very much like Psmith's: fruity, loquacious and tinged with a bemused insouciance. After *Full Moon*, in the Late Period, the style becomes leaner, less complex, a little more jargonistic. I think of the Late Period narrative voice as Bertie Wooster's. Also, the Late Period is marked with an interest in breaking the rules he set up in the Middle Period, an exploration of new patterns: a period of experimentation and change. Could one, for example, imagine even Bertie Wooster joining a club like Bachelor's Anonymous in 1932? And only in the post-War Wodehouse world could we meet a Mortimer Bayliss or Howard Saxby.

As I pursued my admittedly truncated research for this paper, I found that the opening lines of each Wodehouse novel tended to follow the same pattern that his plot structure, characters, imagery and narrative voice did; namely, Early Period: search and growth; Middle Period: standard rich Wodehouse style with a Psmithian voice; Late Period: change and experimentation, crisper style with a Wooster voice.

Besides, it is quite proper to submit the openings of the works of a popular author to such scrutiny. Let us never forget that, while a master craftsman dedicated to his art, Wodehouse was invariably concerned about his sales figures. I always thought he wrote from the heart when, in *Uncle Fred in the Springtime*, he says,

> Shakespeare describes the poet's eye as rolling in a fine frenzy from heaven to earth, from earth to heaven, and giving to airy nothingness a local habitation and a name, but in practice you will find that one corner of that eye is generally glued on the royalty returns.

None knew better than good ol' Plum that when a member of the general public goes to the store to purchase a book, he generally looks at the fly-leaf and then reads the first sentence or so before deciding to buy or not to buy. This was especially the case in the Middle Period when so many of his books were initially serialized, and it was so important to grab the reader as she flipped through her *Saturday Evening Post* or *Colliers*, competing, as he was, not just with other writers, but with the advertisements as well.

So in writing, re-writing, and polishing his works, Wodehouse certainly gave especial care to that opening, hoping to have something to grab his prospective customer and persuade the honest fellow to part with some hard-earned cash for the latest Bertie or Blandings story, thereby keeping our favorite author in those two basic necessities of life: tobacco and golf-balls.

Bill Townend makes this point in *Performing Flea*:

> I had always thought that if there was one thing he excelled in more than another it was the way he began his stories. As a reader I felt that my attention and interest were captured from the very first sentences.

He then quotes the opening page of *The Luck of the Bodkins*, which others (Richard Usborne among them, I believe) have said is Wodehouse's very best opening sentence. While certainly a finely constructed sentence and effective in keeping one's attention and making one want to read further, I personally think it was his second best, but it is still a good place to begin:

> Into the face of the young man sitting on the terrace of the Hotel Splendide at Cannes there crept a look of furtive shame, the shifty hangdog look which announces that an Englishman is about to talk French.

Luck of the Bodkins is, of course, a vintage Wodehouse, written in 1935, the heart of the Middle Period, and I think we know right from this opening that we are in for a treat.

But I also think the sentence misses something in that it does not flow smoothly—there's that considerable pause after "furtive shame." Other than that, however, it is quite delightful. Notice how the first half of the sentence is so like a camera reverse zoom: it begins with a tight close-up of a face and pulls out so we see that it is the face of a young man, then we see that he is sitting, then pulling out more that he is on a terrace; farther, the Hotel Splendide, and now the camera is all the way back, and we see the coastline of France and realize we are in Cannes; suddenly now we are back at the face and recognize the look of furtive shame. That's quite a good expression too, "furtive shame." Not the open shame of a man who has already done something wrong, but the furtive shame of someone who is about to do so. It, along with hangdog look, is also a nice description of how just about every male in this story looks from beginning to end, from Monty Bodkin, here about to talk French, later trying to hide his erstwhile romance with Lottie Blossom from both Ambrose Tennyson and Gertrude Butterwick, to Ikey Llewellyn, the most incompetent smuggler on earth, to Reggie Tennyson, about to start work in Montreal but about as suited for labor as Bertie Wooster is for matrimony, and finally to Ambrose Tennyson, who through no fault of his own, is not Alfred Lord Tennyson.

So here we have a nice intricate sentence that sets the scene, amuses us, and gives us a good central image for all the male characters of the novel. Truly the work of a mature Wodehouse. Notice too how the sentence flows in a nice rhythm, then hits a spondee foot—two stressed syllables—as the joke comes at the end. Let's hear it again:

> Into the face of the young man sitting on the terrace of the
> Hotel Splendide at Cannes there crept a look of furtive shame;
> the shifty hangdog look which announces that an Englishman
> is about to talk French.

Parenthetically, there is another thing about this sentence that I find especially appealing. We know that Wodehouse himself spent much time on the French coast and was certainly called upon to "*parlez-vous*" a bit. So we are aware that he himself has been tortured by the exact emotion that is wringing the soul of Monty Bodkin in this opening sentence.

Of course, such delightful bon mots as this did not flow easily from the pen of young Wodehouse. Now I know that Wodehouse himself expressed dismay at critics or scholars casting too close an eye at his early works as he wrote to Bill Townend complaining about George Orwell:

He is apt to take some book I wrote in 1907 and draw all sorts of portentous conclusions from it. Dash it all, in 1907 I was practically in swaddling clothes and it was extremely creditable to me that I was able to write at all.

Be that as it may, it is still a worthwhile experience glancing back, if only briefly, at those early years. However, out of deference to Wodehouse's feelings (not to mention my limit on time) I will keep it short.

During his apprenticeship, Wodehouse was clearly more interested in getting his pre-adolescent readers into the story as quickly as possible, as this opening from *Head of Kay's* shows:

> "When we get licked tomorrow by half-a-dozen wickets," said Jimmy Silver, tilting his chair until the back touched the wall, "don't say I didn't warn you."

Wodehouse said it best: swaddling clothes. Only later, in *Mike*, does he bother to try to set the stage at all, and even then, it is done without much panache:

> It was a morning in the middle of April, and the Jackson family were consequently breakfasting in comparative silence. The cricket season had not begun, and except during the cricket season they were in the habit of devoting their powerful minds at breakfast almost exclusively to the task of victualing against the labors of the day.

In fact, for the remainder of the Early Period, Wodehouse seems to be torn between getting the reader into the story as quickly as possible and setting the stage properly. He expresses this concern at the opening of his 1919 novel, *A Damsel in Distress*. Although Wodehouse was by then an author of stature and experience—having written seventeen novels, several of which had been serialized in the *Saturday Evening Post*—he was clearly still having difficulty resolving this dilemma. But at least he feels comfortable enough to let his readers in on it:

> Inasmuch as the scene of this story is that historic pile, Belpher Castle, in the county of Hampshire, it would be an agreeable

task to open it with a leisurely description of the place, followed by some notes on the history of the Earls of Marsh-
moreton, who have owned it since the fifteenth century. Unfortunately, in these days of rush and hurry, a novelist works at
a disadvantage. He must leap into the middle of his tale with
as little delay as he would employ boarding a moving tram-
car. He must get off the mark with the smooth swiftness of a
jack-rabbit surprised while lunching. Otherwise people throw
him aside and go out to picture palaces.

As with so many of Wodehouse's stylistic signatures, the answer
to this dilemma comes in the composition of *Leave it to Psmith*. While
written in the third person, the narrative voice of this novel is very
much Psmith's own, and this voice continues to narrate all but the
Bertie and Jeeves stories for the next twenty years. Psmith's way out
of any dilemma is to mix story or description with humor. I think the
beginning of *Leave it to Psmith* can be considered the first truly humorous opening:

> At the open window of the great library of Blandings Castle,
> drooping like a wet sock, as was his habit when he had nothing
> to prop his spine against, the Earl of Emsworth, that amiable
> and bone-headed peer, stood gazing out over his domain.

Here we have the stage being set, while but moments away from the
story's opening, and we are thoroughly entertained by a humorous description of Lord Emsworth. I particularly like that "drooping like
a wet sock" image. It was Evelyn Waugh, I believe, who, when chal-
lenged to defend his statement that Wodehouse was the Master of
English Literature, declared that such a title rightly belonged to any
writer who can generate three completely original similes per page.
With *Leave it to Psmith*, we have a beautiful example of such mastery
with the opening line.

We have also clearly abandoned any pretension to realistic char-
acterizations, another sign of the Middle Period. Lord Emsworth was
described in *Something Fresh*, you may remember, as "dreamy" and "ab-
sent-minded." In this second Blandings story, right from the get-go

Wodehouse drops all pretense of Emsworth being reasonably senescent and has downgraded him to absurdly "bone-headed." And that is significant, for his bone-headedness becomes the key to several plot twists later on. Wodehouse is now using his openings not just to entertain, or set the scene or mood, but also to foreshadow.

If complex sentences with a lot of humor can be considered the hallmark of the Middle Period, then Wodehouse gives us this in spades in his first full Middle Period novel, *Sam the Sudden*. Here are the first four sentences of *Sam the Sudden*. Sit back. This will take a while.

All day long, New York, stewing in the rays of a late August sun, had been growing warmer and warmer, until now, at three o'clock in the afternoon, its inhabitants, with the exception of a little group gathered together on the tenth floor of the Wilmot Building on Upper Broadway, had divided themselves by a sort of natural cleavage into two main bodies—the one crawling about and asking those they met if this was hot enough for them, the other maintaining that what they minded was not so much the heat as the humidity.

The reason for the activity prevailing on the tenth floor of the Wilmot was that a sporting event of the first magnitude was being pulled off there—Spike Murphy, of the John B. Pynsent Export and Import Company, being in the act of contesting the final of the Office Boys' High Kicking Championship against a willowy youth from the Consolidated Eyebrow Tweezer and Nail File Corporation.

The affair was taking place on the premises of the former firm, before a small but select audience consisting of a few stenographers, chewing gum, some male wage slaves in shirt sleeves, and Mr. John B. Pynsent's nephew, Samuel Shotter, a young man of agreeable features, who was acting as referee.

In addition to being referee, Sam Shotter was also the patron and promoter of the tourney; the man but for whose vision and enterprise a wealth of young talent would have lain undeveloped, thereby jeopardizing America's chances should an event of this kind ever be added to the programme of the Olympic Games.

Well. If it weren't for the humor, we might think we were deep into something by Henry James. Perhaps he overdid it a little here—certainly no other opening is quite this prolix—but I think that penning sentences of this complexity with a lot of humor is very much the work of a Master.

There is of course a lot of subjectivity in deciding what is a good opening and what is less than good, and you may notice a prejudice on my part for complex sentences with humorous squibs or nifties buried within—and I may say that I think such structure is the most compelling opening—but an opening sentence need not be terribly elaborate nor riotously funny to be considered, in my opinion, a great opening. One of my very favorite openings is that of *Summer Lightning*. In fact, it was while contemplating *Summer Lightning* that I realized that there is a bit of a problem defining exactly how many sentences comprise an opening. I tried to make the distinction objective by limiting this review to the opening sentence only, but *Summer Lightning*—and most of the Bertie Wooster books—made that impossible. I don't think the first sentence by itself is always a complete thought, and I tried whenever possible to keep the opening short, but intelligible. With *Summer Lightning*, as with others, it is the entire first paragraph. Once again, this novel has a singularly simplistic opening sentence and paragraph, but no less beautiful for all that:

> Blandings Castle slept in the sunshine. Dancing little ripples of heat-mist played across its smooth lawns and stone-flagged terraces. The air was full of the lulling drone of insects. It was that gracious hour of a summer afternoon, midway between luncheon and tea, when Nature seems to un-button its waistcoat and put its feet up.

Isn't that nice? We have here a beautiful metaphor in the third sentence with Nature unbuttoning its waistcoat, but otherwise, the first paragraph consists of four simple declarative sentences that do nothing but say "Summer at Blandings." But can anyone here dream of any other way to say it as perfectly as this?

Here, too, we have the most common Wodehouse opening image: sunshine. It is interesting to note that of the seventy Wodehouse novels, eleven (or about one-sixth) begin with an image of sunlight. Nearly half of the Blandings Castle books begin with sunlight. It is, of course, a fitting image for the Master of sweetness and light, and he uses it extensively throughout his writing. So it is not surprising that it is his most common opening image.

As one would suspect, this image began in the latter half of the Early Period, was used extensively in the Middle Period, and was used less extensively in the Late Period. The first time we see it is in the first Blandings novel, *Something Fresh*, in 1915: the first novel with an opening that not only sets the stage with the sunshine in London, but which utilizes a string of independent clauses to do so. Again, an elaborate opening with a little humor:

> The sunshine of a fair Spring morning fell graciously upon London town. Out in Piccadilly its heartening warmth seemed to infuse into traffic and pedestrians alike a novel jauntiness, so that bus-drivers jested and even the lips of chauffeurs uncurled into not unkindly smiles. Policemen whistled at their posts, clerks on their way to work, beggars approached the task of trying to persuade perfect strangers to bear the burden of their maintenance with that optimistic vim which makes all the difference. It was one of those happy mornings.

There's that nice little joke about the beggars, but otherwise nothing terribly exciting here, and the last sentence, rather than capping it off, is really rather weak. All in all, typical of an Early Period piece. Let us compare this with the Middle Period opening of *Heavy Weather*, which also gives us a view of the London sun:

> Sunshine pierced the haze that enveloped London. It came down Fleet Street, turned to the right, stopped at the premises of the Mammoth Publishing Company, and, entering through an upper window, beamed pleasantly upon Lord Tilbury, founder and proprietor of that vast factory of popular literature, as he sat reading the batch of weekly papers which his secretary had placed on the desk for his inspection.

While perhaps less humorous, this is, I think, far superior craftsmanship. The sun does not just beam on the town, it takes on a character of its own, taking us into the offices of Lord Tilbury, thereby introducing us to one of the main characters of the novel, amuses us, and drops us at the end of the paragraph right into the beginning action of the story, the review of periodicals which will ultimately lead us to reading Monty Bodkin's magnum opus, "Uncle Wiggly to his Chicks."

This opening can be contrasted as well with the opening to *Bill the Conqueror*, which, though published after 1923, was written almost entirely before the publication of *Leave it to Psmith* and, for all intents and purposes, is an Early Period piece. Here, too, we have an introduction to the main action in the very same office with the very same character but much less cleverly done:

> With a sudden sharp snort that, violent though it was, expressed only feebly the disgust and indignation seething within him, Sir George Pyke laid down the current number of Society Spice and took up the desk-telephone.

Typical of the Early Period, it achieves only one objective—gets us into the story. Late enough to be written with a strong ear for sound and cadence (again, that spondee beat at the beginning of the sentence), but lacking the cleverness of having the sun introduce the character to us.

Perhaps Wodehouse himself noticed how often he used the image of sunlight and consciously chose to open a new era of writing by switching to moonlight for his central image in *Full Moon*. But probably not. Still, it is a pleasant irony that the first novel of the Late Period, that period of experimentation and change, is the only novel to begin after nightfall, and it is the reflected, rather than the direct, rays of the sun which introduces us to the characters:

> The refined moon which served Blandings Castle and district was nearly at its full, and the ancestral home of Clarence, ninth earl of Emsworth, had for some hours now been flooded by its silver rays. They shone on turret and battlement; peeped respectfully in upon Lord Emsworth's sister, Lady Hermione Wedge, as she creamed her face in the Blue Room; and stole through the open window of the Red Room next door, where

there was something really worth looking at—Veronica Wedge, to wit, Lady Hermione's outstandingly beautiful daughter, who was lying in bed staring at the ceiling and wishing she had some decent jewellery to wear at the forthcoming County Ball. A lovely girl needs, of course, no jewels but her youth and health and charm, but anybody who had wanted to make Veronica understand that would have had to work like a beaver.

Later on, Wodehouse returns to the sun to introduce his characters in *Service with a Smile*, and rather than insinuating a roll-call as he does in *Full Moon*, he deliberately calls our attention to it:

The morning sun shone down on Blandings Castle, and the various inmates of the ancestral home of Clarence, ninth earl of Emsworth, their breakfasts digested, were occupying themselves in their various ways. One may as well run through the roster just to keep the record straight.

And this he proceeds to do, over the next two paragraphs, introducing us to each of the characters in turn.

But by and large, in the Late Period, Wodehouse is less concerned with a clever or finely crafted opening. Once again, he is ready to get down to the story and not waste any time grabbing the reader. Perhaps he knows that whatever he does, he is going to get his 25,000 or so sales from libraries and faithful fans and not much else. Or perhaps it is because, after the war, his novels were rarely serialized and went straight to publication. But clearly, his novels were getting shorter and his openings less stylistic, as these examples show:

Barmy in Wonderland [1952]:
J. G. Anderson took up the telephone.
"Give me the desk," he said.
They gave him the desk.

Ice in the Bedroom [1961]:
Feeding his rabbits in the garden of his residence, The Nook, his humane practice at the start of each new day, Mr. Cornelius, the house agent of Valley Fields, seemed to sense a presence.

and *Company for Henry* [1967]:

> Fork in hand and crouched over the stove in the kitchen of
> his large and inconvenient house, Ashby Hall in the county
> of Sussex, Henry Paradene had begun to scramble eggs in a
> frying pan.

I do not mean to denigrate nor disparage these books; in fact, I happen
to like all of them very much; it is just that Wodehouse no longer
cared, in the Late Period, how compelling his opening lines were—he
just wanted to get on with the story at hand.

So we see that in the main, Wodehouse's novels begin by either
dropping us directly into the action, setting the stage, providing atmosphere, or telling us how difficult it is to start a novel (see also *Laughing
Gas*). But you will notice that I have omitted any mention of the Bertie
Wooster/Jeeves novels. First of all, Bertie made his debut in the Early
Period, but initially, he and Jeeves were consigned exclusively to short
stories. Now, I have chosen in this review not to deal at all with the
short stories, not that they do not have any exciting opening sentences,
but because there is a considerably different dynamic at play in a short
story. The author is constrained by space. (Not to mention the fact
that this author is constrained by time.) As an example, most Jeeves
stories take place in the country at one or another country estate.
Typically, in a short story, we arrive at the location within two pages,
while in a novel we're lucky if we pull up the main drive by the beginning of Chapter Four. In *Jeeves and the Feudal Spirit*, for example, the old
two-seater doesn't make it through the gates of Brinkley Court until
Chapter Nine. So if one is studying how the Master goes about introducing us to a story, it is only fair to concentrate on that genre which
really allows him full rein. Hence, as I say, no short stories.

But it is important, I think, to realize that all this is happening while
he is writing short stories like nobody's business, and it is in the medium
of the short story that Wodehouse hones Bertie's narrative voice.

Secondly, Bertie, as narrator, does not exactly follow the patterns
established in the other novels, and this is also true for the patterns
we have discovered in the novel openings. By and large, Bertie begins
his stories by telling us about his feelings. The very first Bertie/Jeeves

novel, *Thank You Jeeves*, is typical: "I was a shade perturbed. Nothing to signify, really, but still just a spot concerned."

Clearly here we have no complex sentences, no introduction to the narrative. We cannot tell if Bertie is in London or Brinkley Court, having breakfast, smoking a cigarette, or in the bath. All we know is his mood.

Stiff Upper Lip, Jeeves achieves the same objective with greater style and panache, as is typical of the Late Period, but still we are centered entirely on Bertie's mood:

> I marmaladed a slice of toast with something of a flourish, and I don't suppose I have ever come much closer to saying "Tra-la-la" as I did the lathering, for I was feeling in mid-season form this morning.

And this is true, by and large, of all the Bertie novels. The two main exceptions are *Right Ho, Jeeves*, where Bertie begins, you will remember, by, in Bertie's words, going "off the rails," and *The Code of the Woosters*, which the eminent Wodehouse scholar, Curtis Armstrong, credits with the biggest laugh right off the bat:

> I reached out a hand from under the blankets and rang the bell for Jeeves.
> "Good evening, Jeeves."
> "Good morning, sir."

But there is one other Bertie novel which begins with what I consider his most finely constructed opening sentence. And it is fitting, I think, that *Joy in the Morning* have that honor. Usborne described it as Wodehouse's finest novel, and it is certainly his most finely crafted novel. We all know the sad circumstances that allowed Wodehouse to polish this particular gem to its purest ray. Well, the glow begins right from the first sentence:

> After the thing was over, when peril had ceased to loom and happy endings had been distributed in heaping handfuls and we were driving home with our hats on the side of our heads, having shaken the dust of Steeple Bumpleigh from our tyres, I

confessed to Jeeves that there had been moments when Bertram Wooster, though no weakling, had come very near to despair.

Yes, I do like this sentence. I like the fact that it begins with five— count 'em five—prepositional phrases or independent clauses before we even get to the subject and predicate. I also like that touch of bravado, "Bertram Wooster, though no weakling." I like how he sets the tone by telling us that all is well, but ends the sentence with a note of despair, so we know we have another roller coaster ride before us. I like the uninterrupted rhythm—in fact the first two phrases are almost in meter:[2] "After the thing was over, when peril had ceased to loom."

And it is only after reading it several times that I noticed that for the first and only time in the entire Canon, Wodehouse begins his novel at the end of the story and proceeds to flash back.

Now, if this were a thesis and not just a paper to be read and completed before the audience pelts one with rotten vegetables, this would be a good time to begin an examination of Wodehouse's endings. But I will spare you that. Besides, endings are not nearly as important as beginnings. For one thing, endings don't sell books. And the endings of Wodehouse novels are, I think, a little sad because, after all, when beginning a Wodehouse, one has so much to look forward to, but when finishing a Wodehouse, we are conscious of the fact that the joy is drawing to a close.

So I will leave our study of Wodehouse openings here and let some other soul examine his endings, if anyone should so wish. I have shown Wodehouse's different approaches to opening his novels. I have compared and contrasted a number of examples of his use of imagery, setting the scene, introducing characters. I have shown how the style of each novel's opening, like so many other aspects of his writing, is affected by the period in which he was writing. And I have shown how Bertie's approach to opening a story, as his approach to just about everything else, differs significantly from the third-person novels.

I have also given you my criteria for an excellent opening. Now I leave you to make your own interpretations and determinations. To that end, I have compiled the openings to all seventy novels, which

---

2   Specifically dactylic tetrameter, if you're curious.

is available to each of you as a hand-out.[1] And, if this rather long but erudite dissertation is not enough to earn your applause, I would hope that this unexpected gift will.

---

1   See Appendix for this list.

From the desk of E.
Detroit, MI
18 August, 2017

A Bit of a Jolt

It was with the tongue barely brushing the side of my buccal mucosa that I inserted the words "Wodehouse scholar" as a descriptor when quoting my good friend in my talk on the openings of the novels of P. G. Wodehouse, equating him, in a way, to the great Richard Usborne. It is true that, while Usborne's *Wodehouse at Work*, published in 1961, was the keystone of Wodehouse criticism, Curtis, at that point, had not published a single monograph on the subject (limiting his output exclusively, I believe, to types of tobacco ash and the tracing of footprints), but Curtis had held forth to me personally on Wodehouse in a number of insightful and delightful ways, and the observation he made in re the opening of *The Code of Woosters* was *á propos* to the subj. on which I was speaking, so I felt completely justified in the use of that label for him. Like Humpty Dumpty, I held firmly that a word means just what I choose it to mean.

The use of the phrase, however, had knock-on effects I had not foreseen as Curtis explains in the following article, his first true foray into Wodehouse scholarship. Because the article is rather brief (as these things are measured)—not to mention screamingly funny—it is easy to dismiss the scholarship as "light," which, admittedly, I had done when I first read it. But look closer and you will see some interesting stuff here, including an original insight into how Wodehouse goes about putting a book together and why a "Bertie and Jeeves at Blandings" novel (which every Wodehouse fan dreams about) could never be written.

But of course, the main purpose of the piece was to describe how I had given him a bit of a jolt when he saw his name unexpectedly in print (as if he hadn't gotten used to it by 1998). What most readers did not know was that, in penning this article, Curtis was deliberately returning the favor by submitting it without telling me, knowing full well what my reaction would be upon opening my copy of *Plum Lines* and coming upon it unawares.

You could, as the fellow says, have knocked me down with an f., surprised as I was not only to see an article by Curtis, but one inspired by me! As I picked myself up from the floor, in my mind's eye I could see Curtis smiling smugly to himself at the thought of my reaction on reading the article (or piece, as we writers call it). A nice payback and well-played. But the joke, in the end, was on him, because it took away any modest excuse on his part to demur when I blackmailed him four years later into giving his maiden speech at a Wodehouse Society convention.

MY CONTRIBUTION
TO WODEHOUSE SCHOLARSHIP

Curtis Armstrong

This article was first published in Plum Lines *in Spring 1998.*

Golly, as the Master himself might have put it, what a thrill it was to find oneself quoted in Michael Dirda's excellent piece in the Winter 1997 issue of *Plum Lines*, "Wodehouse and the Critics." For those of you who may have missed it (catching up, as you may have been, on your Kafka and Proust), Mr. Dirda's article focused on Wodehouse as perceived by critics great and small, and there, amid the scintillating bon-mots and penetrating criticisms of such commentators as Maugham, Orwell, Jason, Dudley Edwards and Waugh, appeared the following sentence:

> In yet another learned disquisition, Curtis Armstrong main-
> tains that the opening sentences to *The Code of the Woosters* de-
> livers the biggest, if subtlest, laugh right off. "I reached a hand
> from under the blankets and rang the bell for Jeeves. 'Good
> morning, Jeeves.' 'Good evening, sir.'"

(I would point out that Mr. Dirda mistakenly inverted the last two sentences of the quote, but under the circumstances such carping is unseemly.)

After recovering from the shock of seeing myself quoted in print, I did what anyone else would have done in my position: rushed to the dictionary to find out what "disquisition" means. As I feared, it is a noun meaning "an elaborate exposition of the results of one's inquiries." Now, as tempting as it may be to allow people to labor under the misapprehension that I am an author of learned disquisitions, I feel compelled to admit that I am guilty of no such thing. While bowing to none in my admiration for Wodehouse and possessing a more than passing acquaintance with the Canon, "learned" is not a word I would use in relation to myself, let alone "disquisition." "Another," maybe.

But I can see how the misunderstanding arose. In what was a truly learned disquisition (I have now used this word five times, so it belongs to me), Elliott Milstein quoted me in his essay, "A Study of the Openings of the Novels of P. G. Wodehouse." Mr. Dirda, reading Mr. Milstein's exegesis, probably assumed the author was quoting some hoary scholar, now practically forgotten, living in dreamy and undisturbed obscurity. The truth is even less interesting.

Well I remember, it was in the latter days of September, and the equinoctial gales had set in with exceptional violence. The phone rang, and it was this same Milstein. Always more learned than I, he was slaving away disquisitionally on his paper and was calling for my opinion. I remember telling him that I had always thought the opening sentences of *The Code of the Woosters* were the real Tabasco, and that, I'm sorry to say, was the extent of my contribution to Wodehousean scholarship— until now! Due to one of those strange coincidences that happen so often in literary criticism, a Wodehouse letter has come into my hands which addresses three points raised in Mr. Dirda's article, namely:

(a) What was Wodehouse's favorite among his books,

(b) Wodehouse's view of critics in general, and

(c) The proposed 1955 novel featuring all of Wodehouse's greatest characters in one book.

The letter, written on July 24, 1958 from Remsenberg to a Mr. Simmons (not G. G. Simmons, surely?), begins "How awfully sporting of you to defy that ass on the *Daily Telegraph* by buying *Cocktail Time.* I'm so glad you liked it so much. *I must say I thought it the best constructed of any of my books,* [my italics] but reviewers never notice that sort of thing." Airily dismissive as Wodehouse could be of reviewers, he was clearly keeping his eye on them, for he continues, "The book was published over here today and there is a glowing notice in the *New*

York Herald Tribune. And my publisher has just rung up to say there is an even better one in the *Sunday Tribune* next Sunday, which seems promising." Simmons had apparently brought up the idea of an all-star Wodehouse novel, for Wodehouse says, "Yes, I wish I could do a book of the sort you speak of in your letter. The only trouble with those all-star casts is that it is difficult to give each of the principal actors a big enough part. But," he concludes, "I must certainly try to think up something along those lines." He then says, "My next book will be a book of short stories. I have ten good ones, but I really need eleven, to make the book nice and fat, and I can't seem to get an idea for another. However, there is plenty of time and something may emerge." In spite of Plum's efforts, *A Few Quick Ones* was published the following year with only ten stories.

So there you have it—my contribution to Wodehouse scholarship. Since much of Mr. Dirda's article is devoted to which books are favorites among the critics quoted, I would like to submit my nominations. In my youth, *Right Ho, Jeeves* seemed to me the apogee of Wodehouse's books, with *Uncle Fred in the Springtime* running a close second. Now in youthful middle age, *Summer Lightning* brings home the Silver Medal every time. But my heart will always belong to the first Wodehouse I ever read, *Very Good, Jeeves.*

I may not be learned, but I know what I like.

From the desk of C.
Los Angeles, CA
4 September, 2017

A Legitimate, Businesslike Person

Elliott's 2001 paper on Stanley Featherstonehaugh Ukridge, originally delivered at the Philadelphia Convention that year, is the only one of all his papers that I was unfamiliar with in any form. Privately, he's admitted it is his personal favorite of all the Wodehouse papers he's written. A high bar, in my view, but on reading it, I concur.

I am currently in the midst of a chronological re-read of the entire works of PGW, from *The Gold Bat* to *Sunset at Blandings*. I may not live to complete my task, but it's been educational. I bring this up because having just recently re-read *Love Among the Chickens*, I'm uniquely positioned to add my two cents to Elliott's paper, which draws so heavily on that novel. Fortunately, nothing short of armed force would get me back into that book for at least another three decades, so I'll restrict myself to a comment or two about Ukridge, that Man of Wrath, himself.

Elliott, good capitalist that he is, had considered writing on the Ukridge stories as early as 1991, when he first floated the possibility of a paper on the question of Ukridge and the Theory of Supply-Side Economics. Fortunately, I think, that idea blew over, and some years later, he came up with the idea of a talk which would present the sort of business plan that would have been necessary for Ukridge to prepare if he were to embark upon chicken farming in a legitimate, businesslike way, assuming Ukridge was a legitimate, businesslike person, which, of course, he was not.

To achieve this, Elliott brought to bear his own not inconsiderable business acumen, honed to a razor edge following many years in the pharmaceutical industry, which is not, as they say, chicken feed. Even with this wide-ranging experience, he found the business-plan aspect of the paper, while essential and fascinating, was not in itself of sufficient depth to make up a successful Wodehouse paper—it takes up a little over one page in the final version—so he broadened his scope to make it a more in-depth look at the characters of Ukridge and Corky, the Laurel and Hardy of this delightful mini-saga.

To my mind, Ukridge is one of Wodehouse's great characters. Certainly, there is more to him than his origin story. Indeed, when it comes to fictional heroes, his introduction to the public as a speculative chicken farmer doesn't exactly measure up to, say, Superman's birth on Krypton, to take just one obvious example. As an actor who has played his share of comic scoundrels in his career, I can tell you that Ukridge is the only character in the Wodehouse Canon that I would have truly loved to play. I can see me now, in my yellow mackintosh and pence-nez precariously attached by the wire from a ginger beer bottle, scheming and stealing without a second's thought—this is a role with Curtis Armstrong written all over it. I'd have also been aware that, professionally speaking, this was bound to be a short ride and that I should enjoy it while I could. (As indeed it was: The BBC did produce a Ukridge show in the sixties, which lasted one brief series before vanishing forever. I've never seen so much as a clip of it.)

You see, the biggest problem with Ukridge as a long-running character was he could only keep failing. The minute he actually succeeded, he wouldn't be funny at all. As brilliant a comic character as he was, there is a real element of built-in obsolescence in him, something captains of industry and con men everywhere would appreciate. I expect that by the time Wodehouse was cranking out the last one or two Ukridge stories, he was congratulating himself on having squeezed the last possible drop of juice out of a character who, in less ingenious hands, would've run dry decades before.

I don't make a habit of reading *Love Among the Chickens*—who would?—but when I have, it always amazed me that Wodehouse could have come up with such a great comic character and then have thrown him out with the bathwater, so to speak, of *Love Among the Chickens*; that he thought enough of the novel to re-write it, as if that would help; and, finally, that it would be years before he would see Ukridge's true potential as a minor star, as it were, in a series of low-budget but highly enjoyable studio programmers. Of course, he didn't see Jeeves's potential, either, at first.

I've always loved the Ukridge stories. And I love Elliott's treatment of them because while there has been some critical study on them, there hasn't been enough for me. This paper does a lot to even the score.

STANLEY FEATHERSTONEHAUGH UKRIDGE: HIDDEN VALUES AND FROZEN ASSETS

Elliott Milstein

First given as a talk at The Wodehouse Society Convention in Philadel-phia, PA in 2001 and published in Plum Lines *in Spring 2002.*

A few days ago I came upon an illuminating paragraph in a Sunday newspaper. It was in a column where a lady of fashion dispenses advice to those who consult her about their private concerns. A correspondent wrote "…I am not outstandingly brilliant at anything. I can't leave home as my mother is deli-cate, but I want to do something to earn not less than three pounds a week. I've tried chicken farming but it doesn't pay." The answer was "You might get a job as a reader to a publisher …that or book reviewing."

That explains everything about our literary critics; they are young ladies, not outstandingly brilliant at anything, who have failed to make a success with poultry.

I begin my talk today with the opening of Evelyn Waugh's 1930 book review of a Henry Green novel, not just because I happen to like it and enjoy sharing such things with friends, but also because it shows that Stanley Featherstonehaugh Ukridge is not the only person to have discovered that chicken farming is a very difficult business.

Like Waugh, P. G. Wodehouse was not overly fond of book re-viewers (even though he was, as he admitted in *Over Seventy*, "on the

whole rather well treated by them"). But he did not feel that critical analysis of his early work was appropriate. "Dash it all," he complained, "in 1907 I was practically in swaddling clothes and it was extremely creditable that I was able to write at all." While his Early Period
does have some immature stuff in it, this is, nonetheless, self-effacing
nonsense, and much of his work at that time repays inspection.

By 1905, Wodehouse had established himself as a writer of superb
boys' school fiction. He had published over a dozen short stories and
six books in the genre. He was making quite a decent income out of
it, too, but the market was limited, and he wanted to extend his fran-
chise into the much larger and more lucrative adult market. His break-
through product for this market penetration strategy was the comic
romance *Love Among the Chickens*. The romance involves one Jeremy
Garnet, and the comic subplot is formed from the adventures of his
friend trying to start a chicken farm.

The illustrious Norman Murphy would have us believe that every
character inhabiting the Wodehouse world has some sort of Platonic
ideal in this one, and he makes a compelling case for the likes of Uncle
Fred, Aunt Agatha, and the Empress of Blandings. But there needs
no colonel come from Cumbria to tell us that Ukridge is drawn from
a real-life individual. Every Wodehouse scholar, at some point, tells us
how friend Bill Townend wrote Wodehouse a letter about (as R. B. D.
French puts it) "an eccentric and impecunious acquaintance who started
a poultry farm without capital or experience but with every expecta-
tion of making a stupendous fortune." David Jasen tells us that much
of the character is drawn from another friend, Herbert Westbrook.
Murphy adds a pinch of Townend and a dash of "Shifter" Goldberg,
from the old Pelican Club, while Richard Usborne sees the outline of
James Cullingworth from Conan Doyle's *Stark Munro Letters*. But we
have Wodehouse's own words, in his introduction to the 1920 version
of *Love Among the Chickens* that cleaned up and modernized the earlier
work. It is an open letter to Bill Townend that says, in part,

> I received from you one morning about thirty closely written
> foolscap pages, giving me the details of your friend ----'s ad-
> ventures on his Devonshire chicken farm. Round these I wove

as funny a plot as I could, but the book stands or falls by the stuff you gave me about "Ukridge."

And Townend re-tells the story in his introduction to *Performing Flea*.

Stanley Ukridge makes his entrance in Chapter Two as a newly married man with a business scheme. Here is his, shall I say, business plan, in his own words:

> "You buy your hen. It lays an egg every day of the week. You sell the eggs, say six for fivepence. Keep of hen costs nothing. Profit—at least four pence three farthings for every half dozen eggs. What do you think of that, Bartholomew?"
>
> Garnet admitted that it sounded like an attractive scheme, but, like any cautious investor, expressed a wish to overhaul the figures in case of error.
>
> "Error!" shouted Ukridge pounding the table with such energy that it groaned beneath him. "Error? Not a bit of it. Can't you follow a simple calculation like that? The thing is, you see, you get your original hen for next to nothing. That is to say, on tick. Anybody will gladly let you have a hen on tick. Now listen to me for a moment. You let your hen set and hatch chickens. Suppose you have a dozen hens. Very well then. When each of the dozen has a dozen chickens, you send the old hens back with thanks for the kind loan; and there you are, starting business with a hundred and forty-four free chickens to your name. And after a bit, when the chickens grow up and begin to lay, all you have to do is to sit back in your chair and endorse the big checks."

Of course, as we all know, the entire scheme comes a cropper, not, as Ukridge contends, because the tradesmen who let him have supplies on tick (or "scoundrels," as he prefers to call them) failed to have "the big, broad, flexible outlook" and demanded payment (or, again, in Ukridge's words "worrying me with bills when I need to concentrate"); neither was it because he was "crushed through lack of capital"; no, it wasn't from a surplus of creditors nor a shortage of investors, but rather due to a series of mishaps, including run-away chickens, mad dogs, and an epidemic, not to mention the hired help's habit of eating the inventory and Ukridge's uxorious excesses. So the question is left open at the end of the book: was it a good plan that went wrong, or was there some error with the figures? Let's take Garny's advice and overhaul them a little.

Let us begin with the issue of capital outlay. Can one, in fact, get chickens on tick? Most new enterprises today require payment in advance, or, if you are lucky, net thirty-day terms. Usual cost of unpaid invoices run anywhere from one percent to two-and-a-half percent per month. But things were looser in 1905, and, as it turns out in the story, Ukridge has no problems getting his hens with no money down and no declared interest rate. Mark one for "the big, broad, flexible outlook."

Next, production. Ukridge makes a small error in his estimate of output. Chickens do not lay one egg per day every day of the year. They often miss a day, and they do not lay while molting. On average, they actually lay about two hundred times a year. So let us say we are able to establish our egg factory more or less as Ukridge lays out in his business plan: we are able to create one hundred and forty-four hens each churning out two hundred eggs a year, all with no expenditure of working capital.

Now let us look at the revenue side. Ukridge says that six eggs bring five pence in revenue. (By the way, I checked it out, and that indeed was the retail price of eggs in 1905.) With one hundred and forty-four hens churning out 28,800 eggs a year total, that would yield £100 a year. In 1905, one pound had the purchasing power of £61 today, so that £100 would be about £6,100 today or about $8,750 at current exchange rates. Not bad, but hardly the big checks Ukridge was looking forward to. But even this meager sum is more than could be reasonably expected.

The heart of any business plan is the marketing plan, and Ukridge has none. Without a distribution network or means of gaining a retail trade, Ukridge would actually have to sell his eggs at a wholesale price. Since the five pence price is the retail price of eggs, and wholesale is usually little more than one half retail, Ukridge would, in fact, clear only about $4,500 before expenses.

Ukridge makes light of his expense side. His exact words are "no expenses" though he seems to expect the cost of a farthing per six eggs or about £5 a year. It seems unlikely that one can maintain a chicken farm for so little. While chicken feed is famously inexpensive, still it must be purchased. At two farthings the dozen and two hundred eggs per year, Ukridge is estimating a cost of eight-and-a-half pence per year per chicken. This seems a little low, but as I was unable to locate a price for chicken feed in 1905, we'll give Ukridge the benefit of the doubt. There are, however, other expenses to running a chicken farm.

It is not uncommon for excessive overhead to sink a new venture. To Ukridge's credit, it seems that the chicken farm itself did come rent-free (they were borrowing it from a friend of his wife's), at least for a time. But one can hardly count on that continuing indefinitely. Also, the conditions under which the handyman, Beale, and his wife worked are a little mysterious, but there is mention in the book that they were expecting wages. Then there is the cost of getting the eggs to market, not to mention loss from damages FOB. The most conservative estimate for total annual expenses would be about £20. This would leave Mr. and Mrs. Ukridge with about $2,500 in today's money to live on. One can see why chicken farmers are encouraged to become book reviewers. There is, sadly, no money in chicken farming. Ukridge's first great business never had a chance.

So what ventures follow the doomed chicken farm? After all, Stanley Ukridge would not be the first person in history to wind up a success after an initial flop. Henry Ford, Alfred Nobel, and Walt Disney spring to mind as examples of financial titans who began with failure.

It's hard to say what Wodehouse had in mind for Ukridge at this point—no Ukridge stories immediately followed *Love Among the Chickens*—but Wodehouse himself was developing a business sense, as this was the first time he used a literary agent. In economic theory, agents provide added value by increasing the market value of the person they represent by an amount greater than their commissions. For Wodehouse, in this particular case, it did not quite work out that way; his American agent stole the copyright from him. Perhaps that is why seventeen years pass before Ukridge makes another appearance.

In 1923, Wodehouse began work on a new series of short stories based on the earlier character. Jasen says that in writing *Ukridge's Dog College*, "the going had not been easy." We can see this in a letter Wodehouse wrote to Bill Townend in May, 1923:

> I had to rush that story in the most horrible way. I think I told you that *Cosmopolitan* wanted it for the April number, and I had about five days to deliver it and got it all wrong and had to write about 20,000 words before I got it set. And then when I reached Palm Beach, I found that the artist had illustrated a scene which was not in the final version, and I had to add a new one by telephone!

Much of the language in this initial story is taken directly from the earlier novel, but the character of S. F. Ukridge has changed significantly. One may say that he bears less resemblance to his earlier persona than even Bertie Wooster does to Reggie Pepper. For one thing, his wife, the pitiful Millie, is as if she never were. I think Wodehouse ditched her mostly because having such a sweet innocent forever tied to a man like Ukridge brings a note of pathos disturbing to the comic atmosphere. The famous yellow Mac, the pince-nez with ginger beer wire, his acquisitive habits and exclamations of "Old Horse," "Laddie," and "Upon My Sam" all make their appearances.

Wodehouse wrote the first eight stories in quick succession. He was very pleased with the series, and he planned to marry Ukridge off in the last story of the series—oddly enough, to a girl named Millie—and that would be an end of him. But Wodehouse wanted him back, and, once again, a Mrs. Ukridge would be an impediment, so, immediately after *Ukridge Rounds a Nasty Corner*, wherein she appears, Millie Secundo disappears as quietly as did Millie Prime. Corky did, after all, refer to Ukridge as "the sternest of bachelors." In fact, the Ukridge saga is unique in the Wodehouse Canon in that it practically never has a love interest.

These ten stories are published one a month in the *Strand* and *Cosmopolitan*. This, mind you, at the same time *Leave it to Psmith* is running in the *Saturday Evening Post*. The swaddling clothes are definitely gone;

this is right at the beginning of his Middle—or Vintage—Period. And can you imagine what the fellah is raking in?

Wodehouse, that is, not Ukridge. Ukridge is still the hapless capitalist, jumping into a new, doomed hare-brained venture every month, but there is a subtle change in the nature of his business plans.

Tony Ring and Geoffrey Jaggard are quite right in listing these plots in their wonderful *Millennium Wodehouse Concordance* not as plans or ventures, but as "schemes." That is what they are at best. At worst, they are nothing but scams. The *Concordance* lists the following:

> Running a chicken farm and running a duck farm from *Love Among the Chickens*.

Well, we've already delved into the chicken farm and whilst Stanley does leave us contemplating the duck farm, it is unlikely that it ever got off the ground. Ducks are far more expensive to keep, and there is a much smaller market for their eggs. I think it is safe to say that we can retire the Ukridge of 1905 at this point and bid him farewell. The Ukridge we want to examine is the one from the short stories. His schemes are:

> Training dogs for the music-hall stage
> Taking out subscriptions for accident insurance in the name
>   of a predestined victim
> Managing Battling Billson, the fighter (twice) [actually three
>   or four times, depending how you look at it]
> Selling seven hundred tickets to his aunt's Pen and Ink
>   Club dinner
> Turning his aunt's place into a hotel
> Turning it into a gambling den [technically, that was Oakshott,
>   the butler, though Ukridge thought up the scheme]
> Holding a flag day in support of himself

And three left out of the *Concordance*: going into business with an established book-making firm, acting as front man for a fencing operation of stolen furniture, and selling a snake-oil medicinal called Peppo.

If we look at these schemes narrowly, only two even come close to being possible business ventures: managing Battling Billson and being a bookie. Now, in any business start-up, it is necessary for the entrepreneur to provide value in the form of capital, expertise, or good will. In the case of Battling Billson, Ukridge adds none of these. In the case of the book-making enterprise, he presumably adds good will by providing a larger customer base, and one could argue that it was not his fault that one of his friends bankrupts the business with a lucky bet.

But there you have it. The Ukridge of *Love Among the Chickens* is a naïve, foolish businessman, but the Ukridge of the short stories is nothing but a scam artist. Where in Ukridge do we find what Warren Buffet calls "hidden value"? In other words, where is a Ukridge we can know and love?

Well, "know," of course—at least I would hope that everyone here has at least dipped into a Ukridge or two—but "love"? Is that possible? It is for Usborne: he says so on page eighty-eight of his great opus, *Wodehouse at Work*. On the next page, however, he says, "Ukridge is a thief, a blackmailer, a liar and a sponge. He alternates self-glorification with self-pity...Ukridge is a total immoralist, and he dulls the moral sense in others. He is totally selfish." Nowhere, however, does Usborne explain how one can love such a character. David Jasen claims that Ukridge was Wodehouse's favorite character, but he does not say where he got this or why it should be so.

Other Wodehouse characters whom we cherish in a fictional context may not be ideal friends in the flesh—certainly one is better off without a Bingo Little in one's life—but there is something charming or loveable about them. This is not so with Ukridge. Other than the fact that he is universally loved by all canines, he hasn't one redeeming quality. If he existed in real life, is there any one of us who not run like a hare from such a man? So why does he endure?

Whilst I here draw frequently on Usborne's superb chapter on Ukridge, I cannot agree with the theory he offers for Ukridge's appeal. Usborne says that all of Ukridge's friends are old school chums, and that makes him family, and he must be rescued:

> This gives the reader a rewarding sense of security. He feels able to laugh the louder when Ukridge falls because he knows Ukridge must be put on his feet again, and all will be well, not only with Ukridge, but with his own old-school conscience.

I don't think this is valid. If so, one would feel the same about G. D'arcy "Stilton" Cheesewright and Oofy Prosser, for example, which we do not. No, we laugh when Ukridge falls because he deserves it.

To understand the endurance of Ukridge, we need to look past the main character at the stories themselves. They fall into a genre that Frances Donaldson calls "the situation short story." The other types of story in this genre are the Mulliner stories, the Golf stories, and the Drones Club stories. What these sagas have in common is the use of a narrator who is only marginally part of the action, if he takes part at all. (At first blush it would seem that the Bertie Wooster stories should fall into this category because he too is a first-person narrator, but they don't really as Bertie is always at the center of his stories, even when he is not the love interest, which, after a few early romances, he will never again be. It is because Bertie and Jeeves are so central that they made the transition to novels while none of the other narrators did.)

The narrative voices of these sagas are very similar and are drawn primarily from W. W. Jacobs's night-watchman stories. The narrative voice and story structure closest to this earlier narrator is the golf stories' Oldest Member. Like the night-watchman, he is an older, wiser member of the society of individuals about whom he reports; he is rarely a participant in the story except so far as providing the role of advisor or being placed where he can observe the action, and he is telling his story to someone who is only listening politely because, well, he really has nothing else to do. The Oldest Member, like all Wodehouse narrators, tells stories of loves lost and regained, but the context is always the golf course.

When some action or piece of news pops up in the bar or smoking-room of the Drones Club and various members discuss the situation, we know that one of them will soon have some relevant story to tell. The narrative voices of all those Eggs, Beans, and Crumpets are similar to the Oldest Member's, though there is a touch of a Wooster-like vernacular.

Mr. Mulliner is, of course, the narrator of his stories, but there is another dimension to Mulliner narration not found with the Oldest Member or the Drones Pieface, besides his having a name.

There is a free association test that was once very popular amongst psychologists, where one says a word and the patient is supposed to say the first thing that comes into his mind. Try this sometime at a Wodehouse Society meeting, and, upon saying the word "Mulliner," the most frequent response is likely to be something like "cousin" or "nephew" or "family." Of course, it is always possible to get "Hot Scotch and Lemon" or "Postlethwaite," but you know what I mean. What you will not get, but you should, would be the word "liar."

The first Mulliner story is called "The Truth about George," and the irony of the title is in Wodehouse's calling deliberate attention to the fact that there is not a word of truth in it. The pub is called the Angler's Rest for a reason: this is a fish story; Mulliner is making the whole thing up. Even if you cannot get it from the several subtle clues dropped in the first couple of stories, we know it because Wodehouse tells us so in his introduction to the *The World of Mr. Mulliner*. He says he deliberately made Mr. Mulliner a fisherman so that "[his] veracity would be automatically suspect."

But over time, as the saga develops and as various relations put in encore presentations, an aura of reality surrounds the Mulliner clan, and so we all begin to believe in these lies. Even Wodehouse later forgot his original intent on at least two occasions. I seem to recall an article in one of our many societies' learned journals that actually plotted the Mulliner family tree. The sad reality is, however, that in Wodehouse's world, in the world of the Angler's Rest, there is no George, no Adrian, no Sacheveril Mulliner, no Honeysuckle Cottage or Bludleigh Court, no Buck-U-Uppo, no Nodders, and no Webster, for there are no other Mulliners, either in Hollywood nor Tottenham Court Road. Mr. Mulliner is alone in the world.

But I digress.

So the narrative voice and structure of the Drones, Mulliner, and Golf stories, while differing somewhat in tone or nuance, are essentially the same.

Now one concedes that Mr. Mulliner has a terrific imagination and is a wonderful spinner of yarns; the Oldest Member, too, is an excellent raconteur, and the Drone who tells us about the antics of Freddie Widgeon, Barmy Phipps and the other idiots of the club has a nice way with a phrase and a good sense of timing, but, as stylists, none of them hold a candle to the chronicler of Ukridge's disreputable career.

Corky's stories differ from the other three narrators, not just in their lack of love interest, but most obviously in their subject. The others, whilst they may have their favorites, nonetheless have a variety of different characters about whom they report. Corky has only Ukridge. So as we delve into each new Ukridge story, we may not know the scam, we may not know the girl, we may not know whether it will end ill or well, but we know it will be about Ukridge.

The most significant difference, however, is in the nature of the narrative voice. The narrators of the other three sagas are individuals whom one happens to come upon, and they just begin talking. The context of the story is that the narrator is telling it, verbally, to some luckless individual passing by. The Ukridge stories are not presented as spoken, but rather (like Bertie Wooster's stories) as written, but, unlike Bertie, this narrator is a writer by profession. Corky isn't talking to someone—he is penning these stories, and not just for his own amusement; it's with an eye toward publication and, probably, much needed money. In a way, he tells us so in the beginning of the very first story, "Ukridge's Dog College":

> "Laddie," said Stanley Featherstonehaugh Ukridge, that much-enduring man, helping himself to my tobacco and slipping the pouch absently into his pocket, "Listen to me, you son of Belial."
> "What?" I said, retrieving the pouch.
> "Do you want to make an enormous fortune?"
> "I do."
> "Then write my biography. Bung it down on paper, and we'll split the proceeds."

I think this is a fabulous introduction. Here is true value and economy of language. The initial descriptor, "that much-enduring man," will be filled out before long, but what a deftly elegant first brush-stroke to the portrait! (Later, more often, the brush is harder: "that man of wrath," or even "that chronically impecunious man of wrath" will be the opening appositive).

We are also, before the first sentence is over, introduced to Ukridge, the pincher of other people's things. We learn that the "I" of this story won't let him pinch his, if he can stop it. We see that Ukridge's idea for making lots of money involves someone else doing the work. We know the two men are good friends—one would not call an acquaintance "you son of Belial." We easily infer that both men are impecunious, even if we don't, at this point, know that one is more chronically so. And, as I said, we learn why these stories are being written. And all in fifty-eight words. That Corky sure knows how to write! Well he should, of course; he is, as Usborne says, the young Wodehouse. In fact, in that same letter to Townend I quoted earlier, Wodehouse, discussing the action in one of the stories, actually refers to the narrator as "I" and "me," as if he, Wodehouse, were Corky.

Corky's narration consistently displays the extra value of a professional writer, but as Usborne points out, there is also the dividend that Corky, as a writer, can truly speak for Wodehouse:

> Keep half an eye on Corky. He is really a very interesting background character. He is modest and amusing about his go-anywhere-write-anything trade of Pleasing Editors, but perfectly sure that this is the work he wants to be in. He is fallible and flatterable...His description of the Pen and Ink dance in "Ukridge sees Her Through" has, below its alert descriptions of sound, smells, gilt chairs and potted palms, a cold anger. Here for the first time Wodehouse rolls his sleeves up against the Phonies of the Pen.

You remember the scene. Corky is covering the dance for a Society paper. Ukridge's formidable Aunt Julia is the president of the club. This story takes place after she's had Corky coldly removed from her house for gaining admission under false pretenses.

> The dance of the Pen and Ink Club was held, like so many functions of its kind, at the Lotus Room, Knightsbridge, that barrack-like building which seems to exist only for these sad affairs. The Pen and Ink evidently went in for quality in its membership rather than quantity; and the band, when I

arrived, was giving out the peculiarly tinny sound which bands always produce in very large rooms that are only one-sixth part full. The air was chilly and desolate and a general melancholy seemed to prevail. The few couples dancing on the broad acres of floor appeared somber and introspective, as if they were meditating on the body upstairs and realizing that all flesh is grass. Around the room on those gilt chairs which are only seen in subscription-dancehalls weird beings were talking in undertones, probably about the trend of Scandinavian literature. In fact, the only bright spot on the whole gloomy business was that it occurred before the era of tortoiseshell-rimmed glasses.

That curious grey hopelessness which always afflicts me when I am confronted with literary people in the bulk was not lightened by the reflection that at any moment I might encounter Miss Julia Ukridge.

Which, of course, he does, for you see, Corky is more than a mere narrator. While Mr. Mulliner and the Drones Bean are merely the chorus, Corky is often a principal, dreadfully mixed up in Ukridge's little plots, not just tangentially, but right in the heart of them. He opens many of the stories on some adventure on his own, which is only interrupted by Ukridge. Most of "The Return of Battling Billson" is Corky's adventure—Ukridge only comes on the scene when almost half the story has taken place—and, in "First Aid for Dora," it is Corky's confrontation with Aunt Julia—sans Ukridge—that provides the denouement.

To be fair, much space in the Ukridge stories is taken up by Ukridge himself speaking. Whole swaths of writing come between quotation marks, where Ukridge is either filling Corky in on offstage action or commenting on the situation. But the humor in Ukridge's speech is derived from his predicament; Corky's narration is simply perfect prose.

We have already sampled two examples of his story-telling and descriptive talents. There are many more, just as fruity: Corky's commentary on the pusillanimity of Teddy Weeks, his blow-by-blow of the fight at the Universal Sporting Club, his nightmarish evening with the parrot Leonard, and his horrific afternoon with Flossie's mother and kid brother—the morbid Cecil—to name just a few. The following passage describing the political rally from "The Long Arm of Looney Coote" could almost be a rough draft for the introduction to what is arguably Wodehouse's most famous passage of all, the prize-giving scene from *Right Ho, Jeeves*:

> The monster meeting in support of Boko Lawlor's candidature was held in that popular eyesore, the Associated Mechanics' Hall. As I sat among the elect on the platform, waiting for the proceedings to commence, there came up to me a mixed scent of dust, clothes, orange-peel, chalk, wood, plaster, pomade, and Associated Mechanics—the whole forming a mixture which, I began to see, was likely to prove too rich for me…
>
> The principle on which chairmen at these meetings are selected is perhaps too familiar to require recording here at length but in case some of my readers are not acquainted with the workings of political machines, I may say that no one under the age of eighty-five is eligible and the preference is given to those with adenoids. For Boko Lawlor the authorities had extended themselves and picked a champion of his class. In addition to adenoids, the Right Hon. Marquess of Cricklewood had—or seemed to have—a potato of maximum size and hotness in his mouth, and he had learned his elocution in one of those correspondence schools which teach it by mail. I caught his first sentence—that he would only detain us for a moment—but for fifteen minutes after that he baffled me completely…

Besides Bertie Wooster's, there is little first-person narration in the whole of the Canon to rival Corky's.

But Corky is not our hero; Ukridge is. And when we look at Ukridge's balance sheet, we must say that the liabilities far outweigh the assets. Can we find any hidden value in the man? Usborne thinks we can. He says, "It is a great tribute to Corky/Wodehouse that he can make such an anti-social menace as Ukridge appealing." But I think we can see that it is not so much Ukridge who is appealing as it is the Ukridge stories.

Wodehouse published the first ten stories in 1924 in the volume *Ukridge*; the American edition published the following year was called, for some mysterious reason, *He Rather Enjoyed It*. Everything was properly copyrighted this time, including English serial rights and American serial rights and book rights, dramatic rights and movie rights, not to mention translation rights (including the Scandinavian). Wodehouse wrote several more stories over the next fifteen or so years but with ever decreasing frequency. With *Success Story* in 1948, he clearly planned to end this saga. Ever kindly to his creations, Wodehouse means to leave Ukridge pretty well off, just as he later does Lord Emsworth (eating, you will remember, roly-poly pudding in the library, wearing slippers and a shooting coat with holes in the elbows, Constance thousands of miles away); *Success Story* ends with Ukridge flush with cash, not, alas from any successful business enterprise, but, rather, as the recipient of multitudinous bribes. Nonetheless, Wodehouse drags him out of retirement in 1955 and again in '67. But one is getting tired of Ukridge. It is no mistake, I think, that only one of the stories written after *Buttercup Day* in 1925 is narrated by Corky; the rest are all narrated by Ukridge himself. Corky has no larger part in Ukridge's life than that of a patient listener. Robert Dunhill, Victor Beamish, and Bertram Fox had abandoned him long ago. By the end, while George Tupper may be available for a quick fiver and Corky for a free lunch, they have effectively abandoned him as well. And who could blame them? It profiteth a man nothing to gain Ukridge as a friend if he thereby loseth his shoes, socks, shirts, and dress-clothes.

Stanley Featherstonehaugh Ukridge will be forever frozen in the twenty stories that frame him, an asset, certainly for his creator, providing as he did, rough fodder for some of Wodehouse's most memorable short stories. But the real value of the Ukridge stories, I think we can see, is not in the protagonist, but, rather, hidden in the sublime style and unique character of his Boswell, Mr. James Corcoran.

From the desk of E.
Detroit, MI
12 September, 2017

Quite the Best Talk Ever

The TWS Biennial Convention in Chicago in 2013 was the last one attended by the late, great Norman Murphy. I did not speak at the convention, having given what I thought would be my last talk at the one before, in Dearborn. It was a multi-media presentation on "Automobiles in Wodehouse," on which Norman had helped me quite a bit. We were at the bar, as usual; I was thanking him again for his assistance, and we were reminiscing about talks given at American Wodehouse conventions when he suddenly blurted out,

> "You know, the talk Curtis Armstrong gave in Toronto was, I think, the finest of any talk ever given at a convention."
> "Yes, it was really terrific," I said, "although I thought my talk on Ukridge in Philadelphia was quite good as well, don't you think?"
> "Yes," he replied, "Curtis's was quite the best talk ever. Funny, of course, but very insightful as well."
> "Yes," I said, a little louder (perhaps the old gentleman was getting a little hard of hearing), "there have been lots of good talks at these conventions. The one I did on Imposters, for example, was rather—"
> "I don't remember when I laughed so hard at a Wodehouse talk," he blathered on. "The way he juxtaposed his own personal recollections with similar absurd incidents from the Mulliner stories was just brilliant."

I didn't see any point in continuing. Clearly he was on a roll, and nothing would stop him.

The fact is, however, that he was quite right. And the fact is, also, that I knew it would be true even before Curtis even considered giving a talk. That was the very reason I made sure he did. Here's how.

In 2001, through no fault of my own, I was roped into organizing the 2003 TWS convention. My darling wife, who didn't even read

Wodehouse, came to my rescue, gathered together a small but very capable group of friends, and took care of the whole thing. With one exception. I insisted on organizing the speakers program. For me, the "riveting talks" (as they are called at these shindigs) are the heart and soul of the meeting, and I wanted to ensure that our Saturday line-up would be of a kind to stagger humanity. For that, I knew I needed Curtis.

Not only had Curtis never spoken at a convention before, he had never even attended one. You see, TWS conventions were, by tradition, held in October, as close to Wodehouse's birthday as possible. Curtis always said he couldn't leave LA in October because that was his busiest season. As devoted as he was to Wodehouse, he was more devoted still to working and supporting his family, and October is when actors get jobs.

But, as I was in charge of this particular convention, it seemed to me that I need not be bound by convention (so to speak), so I exercised my prerogative as convention coordinator and scheduled it for August, thus cleverly removing Curtis's lame excuse.

He agreed to come, but still demurred on giving a talk. "What would I talk about?" he wailed. "It's not like I've read him as much as everyone else there. I wouldn't know where to look."

I assured him that most of the people who attend these meetings have read MUCH less Wodehouse than he. He seemed to think the audience was made up exclusively of Norman Murphys and Tony Rings. "Besides," I said, "you've already been acknowledged as an eminent Wodehouse scholar and confirmed it with a learned disquisition in *Plum Lines*."

I pressed him again and again, and, like Caesar in that wheeze of Shakespeare's when being offered the crown, he pushed it away each time more reluctantly. I reminded him that I had moved the convention to a summer date just so he could be there, having learned at my mother's knee the power of guilt as a motivator. The crashing sound I heard over the phone was the final collapse of his resolve. Muhammad Ali claimed he knew he had Sonny Liston in the first round. I knew I had Curtis before the opening bell.

"Besides," I said, "I have the perfect title for your talk. Someone HAS to do this talk and only you can." So I gave him my idea for the title and said, "Now all you have to do is write it."

"Sure," he whined, "as usual, you do the easy stuff and leave the hard part to me!"

"You'll be brilliant, I know."

And, for once in my life, I was right. Even Norman Murphy agreed with me.

NODDERS I HAVE KNOWN:
WODEHOUSE'S HOLLYWOOD AND MINE

Curtis Armstrong

First given as a talk at The Wodehouse Society Convention in Toronto, Canada in 2003 and published in Plum Lines *in Autumn 2003.*

When it was first proposed I present a paper analyzing the Mulliner Hollywood stories to the convention this year, I considered the idea an interesting challenge. I could present my paper from the perspective of an insider of today's Hollywood, looking back on the Hollywood of yesteryear. I could go into the publishing history of the Mulliners of Hollywood, studying each of the stories in turn, revealing the real history behind the fiction, stripping away Wodehouse's brilliant artifice to show the real people behind the masks of Izzy Schnellenhamer or Isadore Levitsky. I could discuss Minna Nordstrom and a time when it seemed people in Hollywood would do anything to be actors and compare it to the Hollywood of "reality" programming, in which people will do anything NOT to be actors. I thought it was a great idea. Shortly after embarking on my project, I opened the new *Plum Lines* and realized I wasn't the only one who thought highly of it. Brian Taves's exhaustive and excellent analysis of the Hollywood of the Mulliners left me with little to add. So I decided to skew my focus less on Mulliner's Hollywood and more on Wodehouse's Hollywood and mine.

But first, a few words on what we in Hollywood would call "the source material." The Mulliner stories are an example of Wodehouse achieving perfection of form, that form being the short double-fiction, or frame story, as popularized by the late Geoffrey Chaucer, to whose *Canterbury Tales* Wodehouse owed some little debt. Mulliner is a taproom Munchausen, and his fabulous embellishments allowed Wodehouse free reign with his literary structures. In no other series of stories did Wodehouse allow himself such dazzling messing about with surrealism. The golf stories were similar in structure and also gave Wodehouse outlets for literary loopiness, yet they remained firmly rooted within the milieu of the links and clubhouses. The Mulliner stories ranged far and wide, and their mise en scène was unimprovable: what better setting than the Angler's Rest—as fishermen are famous for being habitual liars themselves. But Mulliner's fish stories eclipsed them all. There was no class, gender, profession, or country, it seems, that could not be infested by one of Mr. Mulliner's countless relations. A Mulliner could be a banker, a poet, a pastor, or a private detective; he could be independently wealthy or as poor as a church-mouse; it didn't matter. The presence of a Mulliner in a Wodehouse story often as not guaranteed the bizarre and unexpected.

The surrealism in the early Mulliner stories was particularly noticeable because of their setting in traditional Wodehouse country. It was only after fate sent him to Hollywood—and circumstances hastened his departure from it—that the Mulliners of Hollywood made their appearance. Suddenly, Mulliner had a backdrop for his tales that was as fantastic as the stories he was making up as he went along. Previously, it had been a Mulliner whose personality or circumstance brought a kind of heightened lunacy to normal surroundings. In the Hollywood stories, the Mulliners are the sane ones. In Mulliner's Hollywood then—as in mine now—the lunatics are running the asylum and we—the actors and writers—are on the inside looking out, waiting pathetically for someone to come along and shove a bit of lettuce into our hutch.

Immediately following his first visit to Hollywood, Wodehouse set about fulfilling a commitment to write a series of short stories for *The American Magazine,* whose editor had specified American characters in an American setting. There are many who would question whether Hollywood qualifies as an American setting, but Plum used this opportunity to get a little boot in. In Wodehouse's satiric depiction of Hollywood, the romantic spotlight was, as always, on the assistants, the secretaries, the Nodders, the fellow in the monkey-suit—the little people. (And in the case of Little Johnny Bingley, The Idol of American Motherhood, I mean little people in its most literal sense.) But the big shots—especially the stars and studio heads—were obvious targets. These were the people then considered to be America's Royalty.

We laugh now at the idea of Hollywood being anybody's idea of royalty until we remember what England's royalty is like these days. Hollywood would prove to be a perfect "stand-in" for Plum's native land. England had its earls, dukes, its second and third sons of dukes, its daughters of a hundred earls, its valets and gentlemen's clubs: a rich vein to tap. America had nothing similar to point to with reverent pride other than Hollywood. Wealth, privilege, nepotism, inbreeding—Hollywood had it all, plus golf-courses and perfect weather. Despite its protestations, America was no less a class society than England then, and no more so then than today, but within this class structure, there were few cities which were built upon a single universally renowned industry which was itself as rigidly class conscious as Hollywood. The lowest of these classes included the Nodder. The Nodder was not, as might be supposed, entirely a Wodehouse creation. Nodders, under various names, were essential cogs in the wheels of the movie business, without whose wordless affirmations, titans like Louis B. Mayer or the Warner Brothers would be paralyzed into inaction. Nodders sprang, not full-formed from the brow of Plum, but from earlier giants of industry from New York and Boston to Detroit and Cincinnati, who felt naked without five or six Yes-Men on the company payroll.

One of the most interesting evolutions from the dawn of the Hollywood system to the present day has involved the Nodder. At some point, possibly during the early talkies, the Nodders and the Yes-Men evolved into a marginally more advanced animal that became known as an associate producer, assistant director, or development executive, or really any studio or network drone who operates in any capacity under the ultimate decision-making level. Hence, as American society has grown increasingly complex and polarized, the Nodders have gone from being the "untouchables" of the traditional Hollywood caste system to a caste system of their own, in which all Nodders are not created equal.

Nodders today have many names and positions, but for the sake of simplicity, we will still just refer to them as Nodders, for they function in much the same way that Wodehouse's Nodders did. Screenwriters, or scenarists, also play an important role in these stories and were included because Wodehouse knew from experience that screenwriters were always good for a laugh. We tend to think of screenwriters as nearly mythic characters, commanding mind-boggling amounts of money, marrying beautiful actresses, and owning second homes in Colorado.

This was not always the case, certainly not in Wodehouse's day. Screenwriters ranked slightly below Nodders on the totem pole, as Mulliner explains in "The Nodder": "[The Nodder] is a position which you might say, roughly, lies socially somewhere between that of the man who works the wind machine and that of a writer of additional dialogue." The Nodders and the screenwriters in Wodehouse's Hollywood stories represent the bottom-feeders in the studio pond. To put it as delicately as possible, part of their job description involved dining off the excretion of their superiors. I've been a screenwriter, and I know.

> "It is not easy," Mr. Mulliner says, "to explain to the lay mind the extremely intricate ramifications of the personnel of a Hollywood motion picture organization. Putting it as briefly as possible, a Nodder is something like a Yes-Man, only lower in the social scale. A Yes-Man's duty is to attend conferences and say 'Yes.' A Nodder's, as the name implies, is to nod. The chief executive throws out some statement of opinion, and looks about him expectantly. This is the cue for the senior Yes-Man to say 'Yes.' He is followed, in order of precedence by the second Yes-Man—or Vice-Yesser, as he is sometimes called—and the junior Yes-Man. Only when all the Yes-Men have yessed, do the Nodders begin to function. They nod."

Essentially talent-free and just intelligent enough to know which side his bread was buttered on, the Nodder was usually a relative of someone slightly higher up in the industry food chain. This is a matter of perspective, as even those at the top of Hollywood's evolutionary ladder at that time were themselves more like those fish that grow up in caves than anything human. They may've been blind, but they were capable of generating sufficient light to lure in dimmer organisms and devour them. (That much, at least, hasn't changed.)

The flood of Nodders of both sexes in the Hollywood system had, of course, predictable results: Nodders tended to intermarry, producing new generations of Nodders, with progressively diminishing intellectual capabilities. As their parents and grandparents did before them, these hapless hopefuls with production deals in their eyes head for the San Fernando Valley and points west in search of studio heads to be brutalized by. This modern class is known in the industry as "Nodder Fodder."

I have had personally many Nodder encounters in a career spanning over a quarter of a century, but one stands out particularly. This occurred back in the mid-eighties, during the last great Nodder boom in Hollywood. Those were the days when Nodders were Nodders, when you couldn't swing a cat within half a mile of Studio City without hitting one. This was an audition encounter, as opposed to a pitch encounter, but the experience was similar. I had auditioned for a guest appearance on a television series, *Moonlighting*, which would ultimately become a long-running job for me. Having passed the first test, I was brought in to read for the people who really mattered. On entering the room, I was faced with a kind of Pythonesque parody of the Last Supper: A long table, with staff writers, co-executive producers, and story editors arrayed along either side of Christ, or, in this case, series creator Glen Gordon Caron. On the completion of my audition, Caron looked down the table, first to his right, then to his left, and nodded silently. All present nodded back at him. Caron then delivered sentence: two and a half seasons without the option.

Young people often ask me—well, one did the other day—how does one go about becoming a Nodder? There are no academies teaching Nodder technique. Universities don't offer degrees in nodding, at least not intentionally. Well, let us examine him:

Who is the Nodder? The Nodder often started off as a troubled youth, possibly from a broken home, who had fallen in with a bad element and had probably had several brushes with the law. If he had a future, it was either in the studio system or in jail. Of course, as Wodehouse pointed out, that added up to essentially the same thing.

The Nodder's position may have been negligible, but it gave him a sense of community—even if it was a community no right-minded person would want to be caught dead in. In Hollywood nowadays, coming from a broken home, consorting with criminals, and having multiple arrests on drug charges are considered good career moves, but in Plum's day it was still frowned upon, at least officially. A job as a Nodder may have been a young loser's last best chance to turn his life around. You can see a similar system at work these days in the White House.

Some seventy years after their introduction in Wodehouse's fiction, Nodders are still an essential part of Hollywood machinery, even in these tough times. Like their forefathers at Perfecto-Zizzbaum and similar companies, they are keenly aware that their jobs depend on committing to no project verbally until after it has been completed successfully. During the "development process," which can last, literally, generations, a Nodder will be called upon to nod with head-spinning regularity. It is interesting to note that it was when silent film found its voice that the Nodder found his as well. This is, perhaps, to be expected. As films became more complicated, nodding no longer was considered a sufficient or adequate means of communication, if you can call the development process "communication." Today's modern Nodder is allowed to speak. Some, indeed, can be said to do little else. Speaking, though, is not the same thing as committing verbally to anything.

Today's Nodders, like the go-getters of Wodehouse's world, are buzzers—as full of monologue as a nut is full of meat, to use an advised metaphor. But it seldom amounts to more than a kind of white noise, like those rain tapes people listen to to help them fall asleep. Some writers, in fact, find note sessions to be a foolproof soporific. I have had several meetings with Nodders that lulled me into a dreamless slumber, from which I awoke much refreshed.

In *Performing Flea*, Wodehouse tells a memorable story of this sort of thing in his October 28th, 1930 letter to Bill Townend:

> MGM bought that musical comedy, *Rosalie*...for Marion Davies. Everyone at the studio had a go at it, and then they told me to try. After I had messed about with it with no success,

Irving Thalberg, the big boss…worked out a story on his own and summoned me to Santa Barbara, where he was spending a few days, to hear it. I drove down there with a stenographer from the studio, and he dictated an entire scenario. When he was finished, he leaned back and mopped his brow and asked me if I wanted to have it read over to me. I was about to say yes (just to make the party go), when I suddenly caught the stenographer's eye and was startled to see a look of agonized entreaty in it. I couldn't imagine what was wrong, but I gathered for some reason she wanted me to say No, so I said No. When we were driving home, she told me she had had a latish night the night before and had fallen asleep at the outset of the proceedings and slept peacefully throughout, not having heard or taken down a word.

There are some who suggest that some of the letters Wodehouse printed in *Performing Flea* were rewritten and are sometimes of questionable veracity. But no one who has spent any time in a script meeting would have trouble believing that one.

To see a Nodder at his best, you need to see him in a meeting at which he is, as they say, "giving notes." A "note meeting" or "note session" is what happens after a screenwriter has handed in the script that he or she has been laboring over with sweat and sleeplessness for weeks, months, or even years. At this point, the script is handed to a Nodder—often one young enough to be the screenwriter's child—who then, based on a lifetime of experience and vast knowledge of filmmaking, tells the writer what's wrong with it. A good example of the modern Nodder's contribution was when a writer handed in a screenplay, based upon a true story, about the unlikely friendship that developed between a dog and a whale. The Nodder, after expressing the studio's enthusiasm for the project, then asked if the writer would consider changing the whale to a cop.

Something like this happened to my former writing partner, John Doolittle, and me during a note session involving our first sold screenplay, which was interestingly enough based on a Wodehouse story, "Honeysuckle Cottage." As you all know, this famous if atypical Mulliner story involved James Rodman, a writer of hard-boiled detective stories, who must spend a stipulated amount of time in his recently deceased aunt's house in order to inherit her wealth. This aunt was a much-despised author of goopy romance novels, and her aura seems to have infested the house so that everyone who enters it becomes a character from her books. This first experience as a professional screenwriter was a dream come true for me for a while.

The movie was cast—Val Kilmer was to play Rodman, Penelope Ann Miller was Rose, and the late great J. T. Walsh was Andrew MacKinnon, Leila's agent. Our director was Christopher Guest, at the time still best known for *This Is Spinal Tap*. As the son of a peer in the House of Lords, Chris knew Wodehouse and the whole milieu. Our take on this film was that the actors playing Rodman, Rose, and all the other characters in the main story would also play characters in fantasy sequences based on Leila Pinckney's romance novels and on Rodman's noir stuff.

Our first niggling concern regarding it all came when one of our producers objected to a joke in the script referring to the great English actor Ronald Colman. His objection seemed arbitrary and capricious. When pressed as to why we should change the line, he turned vague and unresponsive, finally admitting he had never heard of Ronald Colman. "Couldn't you," he suggested helpfully, "put in an English actor people have heard of? How about Sean Connery?" Sean Connery, we pointed out, was Scottish, not English, and there the matter lay, but the whole exchange could've been written for Izzy Schnellenhamer and no questions asked.

That producer, by the way, has gone on to a highly successful career in Hollywood, producing films such as *Not Another Teenage Sex Comedy* and *The Fast and the Furious* among other productions not based on Wodehouse stories. Worse was when it was decided that the film noir genre wouldn't attract enough of the coveted young male audience to the film, and it was suggested that we change Rodman's hard-boiled detective stories to animated Japanese graphic novels. "But Rodman isn't Japanese," I said, putting my finger on the flaw in his argument at once. Again, a minor cultural victory, but we lost our foreign financing shortly afterward, so the point was moot.

These suggestions underline both the similarities and differences between the Nodder of yore and the ones who infest Hollywood these days. The silent Nodder committed to nothing unless his superior has indicated it is all right to commit to it. The modern Nodder keeps insisting on changes in a script—thereby avoiding commitment to the script as written—until his boss finally reads the final draft and pulls the plug on the project. Wodehouse's Nodder kept his job by not making mistakes; the modern Nodder keeps his by making his mistakes look like the mistakes of a screenwriter who, despite the Nodder's best efforts, can't write a coherent script. Both Nodders will take credit for a successful film—at least in letters home. In fact, the primary difference between the two Nodders is that today's Nodder is actively capable of preventing films from being made at all, which is, I guess, progress of a sort.

Remarkable as they are in their surrealism, the Hollywood stories startle us with their bitterness. These are not the work of Plum, purveyor of sweetness and light. While undeniably funny, these tales are as close to mordant and cynical as Wodehouse would ever get in his career. This is all the more evident when one compares the fictional Hollywood tales to their closest literary sibling—Wodehouse's account of his spell in a Nazi internment camp. There is a certain bizarre irony to the fact that Wodehouse spent part of his first internment in a mental hospital and his second in a town that has frequently been mistaken for one. Whatever the similarities between these two significant events in Wodehouse's life, there were differences, the most obvious being the relative cheeriness of the camp diary as compared to his recollections of his stretch at MGM and Paramount. For example, Plum complained to Bill Townend about his inability to get any work done in Hollywood, while at Tost and Huy he seemed to be churning the stuff out. This beaver-like industry may well have had something to do with not having Ethel around throwing parties every ten minutes, but for whatever reason, he produced, among others, *Money in the Bank* and *Joy in the Morning*. Even the titles sound bright with optimism.

By contrast, the best-known novel to come out of his time in Hollywood was *Hot Water*. Interestingly enough, the time spent in Nazi internment and in the Hollywood studio system resulted in the only two

times that Wodehouse, that most uncontroversial of men, found himself embroiled in controversy. The broadcasts from Berlin resulted in
his estrangement from England for the remainder of his life, while
his famous interview in the *Los Angeles Times* revealing the amount of
money he was being paid to loll around Marion Davies' swimming
pool and play with Maureen O'Sullivan's Pekes ended with Plum effectively banned from Hollywood forever—or at least until they needed
him again and figured everyone had forgotten about the whole thing.

Hollywood's response to Wodehouse's naive revelation of reckless
studio spending was the sort of outraged indignation we remember
from Captain Renault in *Casablanca*: They were "shocked, shocked to
find there was gambling going on here."

Wodehouse would find a very different environment these days.
What reckless spending there is now tends to go into the extensive
computer-generated destruction of the planet or morphing actual
actors into something even less appealing. But Wodehouse's mistakes
stemmed not just from a generally conceded mutton-headedness when
it came to dealing with the press. Nor should blame necessarily be laid
on Wodehouse's naïveté, though that was considerable. Regarding his
Los Angeles Times fiasco, he wrote, apparently without irony, "It was a
casual remark I happened to drop off the record—though, like an ass,
I didn't say it was off the record." No, in Plum's defense, it should be
remembered that any extended period spent in a Hollywood studio,
surrounded by Hollywood people, in that relentlessly charming
climate, can lead to a dislocation from reality in even the shrewdest and
most worldly of people. Your apparent ability to think and move about
freely is a highly deceptive thing in Hollywood. If you're not very care-
ful, your reality becomes Hollywood's reality, which has nothing to do
with what's happening in the real world, as Plum learned to his cost.

It is intriguing, if pointless, to speculate what would have happened had Wodehouse succeeded as a screenwriter in Hollywood. As
Hollywood's product evolved from the romantic and musical comedies
of the thirties (a genre which, we must not forget, Wodehouse helped
create) to more "serious," less stage-based fare in the forties and
beyond, would Plum have evolved with it? Can we imagine Jack Warner,
in this alternate universe, putting down the first draft of Raymond

Chandler's *The Big Sleep* and barking, "Put Wodehouse on it. They went to the same school. Maybe he'll understand it." Or Billy Wilder reading Wodehouse's draft of *Double Indemnity,* in which the Barbara Stanwyck character blackmails Fred MacMurray into sneaking into her husband's room in the dead of night and puncturing his hot water bottle with a darning needle. Not really the same, is it? More chilling than what cinema might have gained in this scenario, though, is what would've been lost to literature: *Louder and Funnier, Thank You, Jeeves, Blandings Castle, Young Men in Spats, The Code of the Woosters,* and *Uncle Fred in the Springtime* might never have been written. *Anything Goes* might not have.

By the fifties, of course, Hollywood waters would have become so culturally muddy—what with juvenile delinquents, giant insects, invaders from Mars, rock 'n' roll, and beach movies—that Plum would've seen the writing on the wall. The work would've dried up. Without the nearly unbroken chain of Wodehouse books through the war years, the popular taste for them might have diminished, had he even been able to write them at all. His well of creativity may have gone dry after years of writing screenplays in Hollywood. Faced with this sort of calamity, Wodehouse may have even become one of those tragic statistics too common at the time and been driven to commit an unthinkable act: He might have gone into television. But there's no point in getting morbid about it.

It is safe to say that Hollywood has changed much in the years since Plum walked six miles a day from his home in Beverly Hills to his office in Culver City. For one thing, anyone caught walking in Beverly Hills these days would be courting arrest and imprisonment. Indeed, in most respects, he would find the City of Angels unrecognizable. But I will leave you with one true story as an example of how much has stayed the same. The story is set in one of the great Hollywood studios, not far from the studio where Plum had labored over *Rosalie.* It was the morning after the Academy Awards a few years back, when *Shakespeare in Love* had won the Best Picture award, beating out a film produced by the studio in question. The top executive was in a staff meeting, surrounded by his top Nodders, everyone licking their wounds. The bitter silence which had fallen upon the room was shattered when the studio head burst out in frustration, "Who the hell is this Merchant Ivory guy anyway?!" It was a cry from the soul that Izzy Schnellenhamer would've understood and a moment Wodehouse would've savored.

From the desk of C.
Los Angeles, CA
27 September, 2017

A Couple of Guys Who Should've Known Better

It was late one evening in September 1981 when I heard a knock at the door of my apartment on E25th Street in New York. It was past my bedtime, but I answered it and found two eager, bright-eyed characters standing there, loaded down with a couple of small valises and what appeared to be a case carrying photographic equipment. One of the men was tallish, the other slightly less so. They were both bearded and wore glasses. I didn't know what they wanted, but they looked like a couple of guys who should've known better. The tallish one was carrying a small pink box with white string around it. I had been living in New York long enough to recognize an Italian bakery take-out box when I saw one.

"Hi," said the shorter of the two. "My name is Carl Bernstein; this is Bob Woodward. We're from *The Washington Post*. Could we talk to you for a minute?"

I hadn't just fallen off the turnip truck, and I knew they weren't Woodward and Bernstein at all, but I liked their moxie. Turned out they were a couple of Midwesterners called Milstein and Fink, which made them sound less like two crack political reporters and more like a Yiddish comedy team. But, whatever, it got them in the door. They just needed a place to sleep for the night, they said. Just one night, they said, then they were headed back to Detroit. Okay, I'm a sucker. I was young once, too. But I frisked them anyway. They were clean.

"Fine," I said, "pull up the floor, make yourself at home." The tallish one handed me the little pink box. I was right. It was some sweet Italian pastry that tasted like they got it off of the "day-old" shelf about three days ago.

They were a little vague about what had brought them to New York, which I appreciated. There was something about these two that made me think the less I knew about them, the better for everyone. They did tell me it had something to do with a wealthy book collector called Heineman. I said I didn't much care who they were grifting. It'd been a long day, and I needed some shut-eye. I told them to keep the noise down, use the ashtrays, and not to leave the toilet seat up. I may leave my socks on the floor, but I'm particular about some things.

They kept the noise down, all right. When I got up the next morning, they were gone. Along with my wallet, my stereo system, and an authentic Crown Derby Tea Service.

I never found out who Heineman was. I just hope he had insurance.

THE NATURE AND THE DEVELOPMENT OF THE IMPOSTOR IN THE WORKS OF P. G. WODEHOUSE

Elliott Milstein

First given as a talk at The Wodehouse Society Convention in Kalamazoo, MI in 1989. Revised and given again at The Wodehouse Society Convention in St Paul, MN in 2009. Published in the revised version in Plum Lines *in Winter 2009.*

Wodehouse makes being an impostor seem so easy, but having been one myself, I can assure you that it requires nerves of steel.

In an introduction to the 1970 Mayflower paperback edition of *Something Fresh*, Wodehouse writes,

> The one thing that might be considered to militate against the peace of life at Blandings was the constant incursion of impostors. Blandings had impostors the way other houses have mice. I have recorded so far the activities of six of them, and no doubt more to come…

Ring and Jaggard, in their wonderful *Millennium Wodehouse Concordance*, come up with a list of Blandings impostors which numbers a staggering nineteen names. One wonders why Wodehouse, while clearly trying to impress the reader with a significant quantity, only comes up with a mere six. We must assume that Wodehouse's definition of an impostor differs substantially from the definition that Ring and Jaggard use.

I would aver that the narrowest definition of an impostor is some-one who presents himself as another real or extant person. With that definition, let's see whom we come up with.

Well first, of course, is Psmith, who in *Leave it to Psmith* comes to the castle as the Canadian poet Ralston McTodd. Next would be Sue Brown, arriving as the American heiress Myra Schoonmaker, in *Summer Lightning*. Uncle Fred shows up in the springtime as the nerve specialist Sir Roderick Glossop. And finally, Sam Bagshott arrives as Augustus Whipple. (Yes, Whipple, not Whiffle, that famed pig specialist having undergone one of those weird Wodehouse name changes in *Galahad at Blandings*.) That's a count of only four. We could possibly add Eddie Cootes, who also shows up trying to worm his way in as McTodd, but, though he fits the definition, it is unlikely Wodehouse was think-ing about him, and even if he was, that would still be only five. Who is missing?

Could Wodehouse have been thinking of Bill Lister? Bill Lister is listed twice in the *Concordance*, once as Messmore Breamworthy and once as Landseer. Both are real people, but there is a little difficulty here. Freddie Threepwood suggests the name Messmore Breamworthy when he and Gally are helping Bill work out the details of his impos-ture, but Mr. Breamworthy is a Vice President at Donaldson's Dog Joy, not an artist, so Bill is not really impersonating him, just borrowing his name. (Also, as Messmore Breamworthy, Bill is never actually invited to stay at the Castle—he puts up at the Emsworth Arms and only visits to paint the pig—so technically he is not an impostor "at Blandings Castle.")

Now, unlike Breamworthy, Landseer is actually invited to stay at the Castle, and it is not Bill's fault that he is tossed out a mere fifteen minutes after showing up. And Landseer was also a real person—and an artist. But while Gally did lead Emsworth to believe that Bill was Sir Edwin Landseer, he backed off and changed his story when con-fronted with Hermione's knowledge that Sir Edwin, though real, was not extant, having long since handed in his dinner pail (October 1, 1873, just to keep the record straight), so it is questionable whether this qualifies as the type of "pure" imposture needed to reach Wodehouse's count of six. (Interestingly, there was one other act on Bill's part that the *Concordance* does not enumerate, viz. his haunting the grounds as an unnamed gardener—complete, you will remember, with Fruity Biffen's beard. I think we have to consider this an act of imposture, especially because of the beard.)

Wodehouse wrote this little introduction right after he finished *A Pelican at Blandings*, which includes Vanessa Polk whom Gally specifically identifies as an impostor before launching into a general reflection on the issue:

> . . . the Polk wench. . .It turns out she's an impostor. It's an odd thing about Blandings Castle, it seems to attract impostors as catnip does cats. They make a bee line for the place. When two or three impostors are gathered together, it's only a question of time before they are saying "Let's all go round to Blandings," and along they come. It shakes one. I've sometimes asked myself if Connie is really Connie.

Hard words from someone who is responsible more than anyone else for introducing these impostors. Anyway, this passage clearly shows that the impostor motif was on Wodehouse's mind a good deal around this time. But as Vanessa Polk is not impersonating a real person, this means Wodehouse's definition must be somewhat more liberal than the narrow one I gave earlier. If, however, we adopt a looser definition, then we open the door wide enough to admit not just Ms. Polk and the Blister, but also Pongo and Polly Pott as Glossop's secretary Basil and daughter Gwendolyn, respectively, and several more, in which case we would surpass the number six and are soon up to Ring and Jaggard's number of nineteen, and possibly more.

We must face the fact that Wodehouse was probably just plucking a number out of the air, choosing his favorite humorous numeral, six (as in "Fiend with Hatchet Slays Six" or "I jumped six inches into the air"). With Ring and Jaggard, we are much closer to the mark. But even that list is not, I think, entirely accurate.

As I mentioned, they left off Bill Lister's stint as a gardener, but my biggest issue with their list comes in the very first Blandings Castle novel, *Something Fresh*. It is odd to me that Ring and Jaggard list Joan Valentine, but not Ashe Marson. True, Ashe does not take a false name

and Joan does, but others in the Ring and Jaggard list, like John Halliday and Vanessa Polk, use their own names. Remember that Ashe is
pretending to be a valet in order to gain entrance to the castle so he
may steal back Mr. Peters' scarab, whereas Joan was, in fact, a real lady's
maid, so which is the greater imposture?

Besides, we must list Ashe as an impostor because Wodehouse, as
narrator, calls him one in the book. Ashe is assembling with the rest of
the domestic staff for the first time preparatory to going in to dinner,
and feeling completely out of place, the narration concludes with, "He
himself, he felt, had impostor stamped in large characters all over him."

And what about Eileen Peavey? I think Ring and Jaggard missed
a trick in leaving her off their list. While Eileen Peavey is in fact the
modern poetess Eileen Peavey, she is also Smooth Lizzie, the sharpest
li'l pickpocket east of the Mississippi. The false name issue is not what
makes or does not make her an impostor. The fact that she writes
under a different name than the one with which she was christened
should not be held against her; otherwise, we must include in our
list of great impostors Jane Austen, the Brontë sisters, George Eliot,
O. Henry, Saki, and a host of others. But she did infiltrate the castle
with a hidden intent, which is, I think, a key aspect of imposture.

But hidden intent alone is not the whole story; otherwise, we must
include Percy Pilbeam, who, after all, comes to the castle pretending
to investigate the pig theft, but is really there to steal Gally's manuscript. Ring and Jaggard do not include him (and I would not either),
although it is curious that leaving Pilbeam out, they include Baxter
merely for pretending to be on a motorbike tour.

Now the point of all this is not to show up the errors of omis-
sion and commission in the *Millennium Concordance*, though correcting
such Wodehouse luminaries as Tony Ring and Geoffrey Jaggard does
engender in one a somewhat smug pride. But we understand and sym-
pathize. Deciding what exactly is an act of imposture and what isn't
can be rather difficult in a Canon so filled with plots of deception,
and one can understand the difficulty they must have had in compiling
their list. Nonetheless, it is worthwhile trying to determine what exactly
constitutes the act of imposture.

Personally, I reject the idea of merely giving a false name as a form of imposture. Surely Oliver Sipperly had no intention of passing himself off as the founder and commander of the Red Army and Commissar of War of the Soviet Union when he gave the name Leon Trotsky in the Bosher Street Police Court. And then there is Ukridge, who is never an impostor, but always gives a false name as an ordinary business precaution. (Oddly, the only impostor in the Ukridge stories is poor Corky, sent by Ukridge to interview his Aunt Julia for the weekly paper, *Women's Sphere*, though he declines to give a false name.) Giving a false name is evidence of hidden intent, true, but imposture must include a motive beyond merely concealing one's identity.

I think that in the Wodehouse Canon, imposture must include one of three motives, two of which are his two great motives for everything: Love and Money. Generally, those who affect imposture for the sake of Love are heroes, while those who deceive for monetary gain are villains, but this rule is not hard and fast. Let us not forget that Psmith, who comes to Blandings in pursuit of Eve Halliday, is also there to steal Lady Contance's necklace; Uncle Fred comes in aid of Polly Pott's romance but also with the intent of extracting money. But neither Psmith nor Uncle Fred can be considered in quite the same league as, say, Dolly and Soapy Molloy, whom we first meet in *Money for Nothing*, infiltrating Rudge Hall, doing their brother-and-sister-Silver-Ring-Oil-shares routine.

What separates Uncle Fred and Psmith from such disreputable characters is that their motives do not include *personal* gain. They are impostors for that third Wodehouse motive—in the words of Joan Valentine (and many who follow)—"the fun of it." Psmith pretended to be Ralston McTodd initially because, after spending some weeks in the fish business, he enjoyed being mistaken for a poet. He had not yet set eyes on Eve Halliday nor formed his plan to follow her to Blandings.

With such motives at the hand of a master plot-spinner, it is no wonder that imposture is integral to so many of Wodehouse's stories. But like all of Wodehouse's special touches, the impostor motif did not spring Athena-like from his head. We see crude elements of it in the early stories, such as "The Man Upstairs," "Deep Waters," "Bill the

Bloodhound," "Extricating Young Gussie," and "At Geisenheimer's," to name but a few.

A Gentleman of Leisure (1910) is a novel greatly under-rated by most Wodehouse scholars, but I think it is the first quintessential Wodehouse novel. David Jasen points out that this is the first humorous story to be set in a stately home in Shropshire, to feature an amiable but dim-witted peer, the first in a long line of Drones, a tycoon, a formidable aunt, a pretty but foolish girl, and a butler. (Actually, the first two items in his list, the peer and the Drone, are one person in the book—Lord Dreever, who is not actually a member of the Drones Club, but he is admittedly a Drones-like character.)

Jasen also leaves out of this list the underworld motif, first introduced here and used to great effect later in *The Prince and Betty, Psmith Journalist, The Little Nugget,* and, later still and in an increasingly more comic vein, in *Big Money, Do Butlers Burgle Banks, Pearls Girls and Monty Bodkin,* and on and on.

In addition to all these standard Wodehouse touches, we also have two very nice, though not fully developed, impostors. The first, our main character Jimmy Pitt, is caught breaking into the police chief's home on a bet. In order to pull off the situation, he must pretend to be a master cracksman. Unfortunately, this is how he is remembered by the characters with whom he dealt that evening. So he continues to pretend to be a master thief, though in order to maintain his cover without actually stealing anything, he explains that he has retired. This is a sort of quasi-impostor because the reason for the deception, the hidden intent, is not germane to the plot, but merely there to force the situation.

The book does contain, however, a very real impostor: a minor character called Hargate, who has insinuated himself into the castle with the object of cleaning up on billiards. Hargate is the first of many characters to come to a country house with the intent of fleecing its inhabitants.

A Gentleman of Leisure, while a great seminal work, is weak in a lot of ways, and there is no doubt that the use of the impostor motif is not as fully exploited as Wodehouse will achieve later.

Shortly after, in *The Little Nugget*, Wodehouse introduces White, the butler, who turns out to be Smooth Sam Fisher, one of many who is trying to abduct the obnoxious Ogden Ford. Wodehouse plays again with this form of deception in *Uneasy Money*, but this time it is the hero who hides his true situation in order to insinuate himself in someone else's home. His motives are only tangentially connected to Love, Money, or Fun, but they are benign, viz. to meet and help the individuals whom he has quite inadvertently relieved of their inheritance. Lord Dawlish even takes on a pseudonym, his own name before he came into his title.

We have already covered Ashe and Joan from *Something Fresh,* which is next chronologically, and, given how singularly rife with impostors the Blandings saga is, it is fitting to note that this first Blandings story is also the first Wodehouse novel in which the imposture is germane to the plot.

But it is in 1917, with *Piccadilly Jim,* that the impostor truly comes into his own. You could not conceive a more intricate impostor plot, nor one so well executed. As Basil Boothroyd would say, "Don't try it. You're not up to it." Here not only is the imposture germane to the plot, it is the plot itself. Jimmy Crocker, feeling that he has made life in London too hot for his poor dad, decides to go to America and, en route, falls in love with Ann Chester. Before he can reveal his name to her, he discovers that she hates him (though she does not recognize him). So, when called upon to identify himself, he gives her a false name.

While in America, she talks him into impersonating himself, so that he is Jimmy Crocker impersonating Algernon Bayliss, impersonating Jimmy Crocker. Once ensconced in his aunt's house, he finds his father there impersonating a butler. Worst of all, he meets an old friend of his, Lord Wisbeach, who turns out not actually to be Lord Wisbeach but, you guessed it, another impostor. Jimmy is, of course, unable to unmask him without unmasking himself, but he is still one up on the crook in that Jimmy knows he is really Jimmy while the crooks thinks he is not. Got all that? Here we have the three motives again, Jimmy doing his bit for love, his old man butling for the fun of it (or the love of baseball), and the ersatz Wisbeach on site to pull a job.

It is several years after *Piccadilly Jim* before Wodehouse returns to using the impostor plot device, and of course it is at Blandings with *Leave it to Psmith*, which we have shown has three impostors, or four if you include, as Ring and Jaggard do, Susan the housekeeper, who is actually a detective.

By this time, Wodehouse had become particularly keen on imposture as a plot device, and from this point on, uses it quite frequently. Even Bertie and Jeeves take their turns at it. Bertie has to fill in as Sippy in "Without the Option," and *The Mating Season* has the delightful plot twist of Bertie going to Deverill Hall as Gussie Fink-Nottle, while Gussie shows up later as Bertie. Catsmeat Pirbright could also be considered an impostor as he fills in as Bertie's valet. In the later novels, even Jeeves comes on stage impersonating, if ever so briefly, Inspector Witherspoon of Scotland Yard in *Stiff Upper Lip, Jeeves* and Bertie's accountant in *Aunts Aren't Gentlemen*, while Sir Roderick Glossop unbends enough to impersonate a butler in *Jeeves in the Offing*.

I have always been fond of *Money in the Bank*'s impostor motif. I don't think Chimp Twist qualifies as an impostor, simply because he uses the *nom d'affaires* J. Sheringham Adair. But here we have the unusual and original plot twist where the owner of the country house that is the setting of the story is the impostor, with Lord Uffenham acting as his own butler Cakebread. It is, however, Jeff Miller who is the real star when he shows up impersonating J. Sheringham Adair. Jeff is very much in the Psmith mold. In fact, he uses almost exactly the same argument in excusing the crime of imposture that Psmith does. Psmith, wooing Eve, says, "What do you have against me when we come to examine it narrowly. Merely that I am not Ralston McTodd. Think how comparatively few people are Ralston McTodd." Jeff, in explaining why Mrs. Cork did not throw him out in learning of his imposture, says, "A fair-minded, clear thinking woman, she realizes what a venial offence it is not to be J. Sheringham Adair. As she pointed out, she is not J. Sheringham Adair herself, nor are many of her best friends."

If we are looking for the Wodehouse locale most densely populated with impostors, it is not, contrary to Wodehouse's own opinion, Blandings; no, we must leave Shropshire and indeed all of England. Hollywood, by its very nature, is a fertile ground for impostors. It is a place where actresses like Minna Nordstrom are really parlormaids, and gorillas are really Balliol men. But here again we get on shaky ground regarding definition. In a place as rife with deceit, deception, guile and impersonation, what can we say really constitutes imposture? If we employ our most liberal definition, then virtually everyone in Hollywood is an impostor, and certainly the novel with the most impostors is *Laughing Gas*, where every domestic servant is an actor, and even kidnappers are really would-be script writers. Brinkmeyer's English butler, Japanese gardener, Filipino footman, and Gunga Din-reciting chauffeur make four. But what about those kidnappers, George, Eddie, and Fred? Other than the fact that Fred was once an extra, we don't really know if they were impersonating kidnappers or were the real thing. Was Eggy Mannering impersonating a vocal coach, or was he really trying to start a new career? And what about our main characters, Reggie Havershot and Joey Cooley? Can we say they were impersonating each other when their souls switched bodies? We are in such a gray area here, we could even say that April June, while wooing Reggie, is impersonating a human being when she is in reality a female dog that rhymes with the word "switch." Like everything else in Hollywood, it is all chimera.

But the Wodehouse novel with the greatest number of true impostors and the most convoluted impostor plot still takes place outside of England, in that other land where deception reigns supreme: France. I speak, of course, of *Hot Water*. Packy Franklyn poses early on as a barber, but that is just to warm things up. Blair Eggleston, writer of stern, stark novels and secret fiancé of Jane Opal, finds himself unwittingly coerced into becoming Jane's father's valet. But the plot really gets going when Packy insinuates himself into the Chateau Blissac as the Vicomte De Blissac by the most ingenious ruse. The Veek, as the Vicomte is known among his acquaintants, while celebrating the Festival of the Saint, gets into a contretemps with his intended host, J Wendell Gedge. Both were sunk rather deeply beneath the Plimsoll line at the time, so Packy takes the advantage of their faulty memories to convince each that he had murdered the other and must lie low, and then proceeds, himself, to the chateau in the Vicomte's place. Once there, the impostors come thick and fast. There is Medway, Mrs.

Gedge's maid, who pretends to be a detective but is in fact Gum-Shoe Gertie, erstwhile and future partner of Oily Carlyle, who himself later arrives as the Duc de Pont-Andemer. When Mrs. Gedge arrives and exposes Packy, he readily drops one imposture for another, pretending to be a detective from Mrs. Gedge's insurance company. But, although there are now two fake detectives, Wodehouse introduces a real one; it seems that Mrs. Gedge's secretary, Miss Putnam, is actually an employee of the James B. Flaherty Agency. And just to round things out at the very end, Mrs. Gedge is blackmailed into accepting the final resolution of affairs after being exposed as Julia, Soup Slatterly's former partner and the sweetest little inside stand a safe cracker could ever have.

So how many impostures is that? I count nine, but I may have missed one.

Of course, the ultimate impostor story in the Canon takes place not in Hollywood, nor France, nor again at Blandings, but in the suburbs of London. "Uncle Fred Flits By," while a short story, and thus by its shorter duration, not really lending itself to holding the record for the greatest number of impostors, certainly has the most concentrated use of them, as it introduces as its main character the ultimate Wodehouse impostor, Frederick Altamont Cornwallis Twistleton, fifth earl of good old Ickenham. Here, to quote Ring and Jaggard, "within a period of what, realistically, could not have been more than an hour, and probably was considerably shorter, there were seven different impersonations." Remember, however, that only four were conducted by Uncle Fred, while the other three were thrust upon the unwitting Pongo. The initial motive proffered by Uncle Fred was simply to get out of the rain, but we all know it was purely for fun. Later, the Love and Money side of it come into play, but only after the imposture is in full swing.

Though Uncle Fred goes on to a great career in imposture, this first outing was the feat he was most proud of, as we can tell from his recitation of the event to Bill Oakshott in *Uncle Dynamite*:

My dear fellow, at the Cedars, Mafeking Road, in the suburb of Mitching Hill last spring I impersonated in a single afternoon and with complete success not only an official from the bird shop, come to clip the claws of the parrot, but Mr. Roddis, lessee of The Cedars, and a Mr. J. G. Bulstrode, a resident of the same neighborhood. It has been a lasting grief to me that I was given no opportunity of impersonating the parrot, which I am convinced I should have done on broad, artistic lines.

In *Cocktail Time,* Wodehouse goes even further, asserting, "It was his modest boast that there was nothing in existence, except possibly a circus dwarf, owing to his height, or Gina Lollobrigida, owing to her individual shape, which he could not at any moment and without rehearsal depict with complete success."

Sadly, though he appears in two more books after *Uncle Dynamite,* he does not impersonate anyone in either (other than two very brief scenes in *Cocktail Time,* one as the fictional Inspector Jervis and the second as secret agent Number X3476). Of course, it would have been impossible in *Service with a Smile,* as he was already known at Blandings, but I think there is another reason. Having married Pongo off in *Uncle Dynamite,* he is alone, and, in Wodehouse, an impostor who is having fun generally is paired with one for whom the experience is, well, not so much.

Pongo's constant mishaps and terror at being discovered are a perfect yin for the yang of his Uncle Fred's classy impersonations and indestructible *sangfroid.* From the train ride to Blandings on, practically all of *Uncle Fred in the Springtime* is a *pas de deux* of Pongo's frenetic pessimism and Uncle Fred's breezy insouciance. My favorite passage that shows this occurs immediately after Baxter informs them he is aware they are impostors:

> Rupert Baxter continued to tap his fingertips together and to project through his spectacles as stern a glare as they ever been called upon to filter, but he was conscious as he did so of a certain sense of flatness. Unmasked Guilt, in his opinion, should have taken it bigger than this man before him appeared to be doing. Lord Ickenham was now peering at himself in the mirror and fiddling with his moustache. He may have been feeling as if the bottom of his world had dropped out, but he did not look it.
>
> . . .

[Baxter] restored his composure with a glance at Pongo. There, he felt, was Unmasked Guilt looking as Unmasked Guilt should look.

Besides Uncle Fred and Pongo, there are many other such pairings. Blair Eggleston's misery is an excellent foil for Packy Franklyn's grand time. Of course, in arranging things thus, Wodehouse is deliberately trying to show Packy as the preferred suitor of Jane. But consider *Spring Fever*, where both Mike Cardinal and Stanwood Cobbold are sympathetic characters, yet Mike Cardinal, impersonating Stanwood, is enjoying himself thoroughly, while Stanwood shows up later, awkwardly and unhappily filling in for the millionaire Rossiter.

It is natural, I think, as we read these stories of imposters and their glorious exploits, to daydream about how well we might pull something like that off if called upon to do so. We see ourselves as Uncle Fred or Psmith carrying the whole thing off nicely with detachment and *savoir faire*. I know I did. By the time I had finished writing my thesis, I had read nearly every Wodehouse book and encountered, as I have now shown you, dozens and dozens of imposters between their covers; each and every time, I thought to myself, "how jolly it would be to go on such an adventure." Then, suddenly, I was called upon to actually do so. Let me tell you: it's a whole different thing when you are living it rather than reading it. Let me share my story.

It was back in 1981, the early days of the Reagan administration. Reagan had begun his campaign of deregulation with, you may remember, the airline industry. One of the early benefits of the campaign was that we were suddenly infested with a number of cut-rate airlines. In the summer of 1981, New York Air had a big promotion to highlight their $49 fare from Detroit to New York. For the first forty-nine people who bought a ticket, they could get a return ticket for forty-nine cents. My friend Ken Fink, never one to pass up a bargain, camped out in the Detroit airport and procured two roundtrip tickets to New York for under $100!

I do not know how many others Ken approached to join him on his metropolitan jaunt before he came to me. I'd like to think there weren't too many. Ken knew well that New York is my favorite city in the universe, and it was nice of him to think of it as a trip for us both.

Now these were lean years for us; just out of school and after the ravages of the Carter years, pickings were slim. Kenny was slaving away as a cub photographer for a not-so-great non-metropolitan newspaper, and I was a traveling salesmen opening new territories for my father's tiny company. Somehow, we could never get our schedules and our budgets to agree on a trip. The deadline for using the tickets was fast approaching, and Kenny's $100 bargain was about to expire into a big mistake.

Then he found a talking point. The Wodehouse centenary exhibit was opening in a week. We could fly in just for the day, catch the exhibit, a play, do some shopping, and fly out. Our friend Curtis Armstrong, then a struggling actor, could put us up for the night. Sounded great.

Unfortunately, a little research showed that the exhibit opened the week I was to be out of town on business. The week after, the tickets were no good. Could I cancel my trip? No. Could Ken take a day off work? No. What to do…?

Now I want you to know that Kenny, may he rest in peace, was a scrupulously honest individual, but when there was something of great import in the balance, he would unbend far enough to pull the old schoolboy trick of not exactly lying, but not really telling the truth. And what Kenny did was this.

He called the Wodehouse centenary and got the secretary for James Heineman, the preeminent Wodehouse collector who was organizing the event. He explained that he was with the Oakland Press (the newspaper he worked for was in fact located in Oakland County, Michigan—not his fault if she thought he was from San Francisco), that he happened to have a photographer and a reporter in New York this Saturday (well, he was a photographer, and I had been a reporter for my university newspaper), and could they get admittance to the exhibit even if it wasn't open yet? Somehow, he was able to create the image of full page spreads all over northern California, and doors were opened, passes printed, red carpets unfurled, and plane reservations made.

We arrived in Gotham bright and early, breakfasted, and shopped. Before our afternoon rendezvous at the Morgan Library, Ken wanted to again go over the plan: remember, we are from the Oakland Press—try to avoid mentioning just where this Oakland is. If necessary, he would flash his quite legitimate Press Pass. Once in a while, Ken would take pictures but say nothing. It was up to me to carry the day. I was feeling more and more like Corky about to interview Ukridge's Aunt Julia.

He gave me a real reporter's notebook and instructed me on a few simple tips. Don't get involved in lengthy discussions on the development of the Drones Club or the difference between Galahad and Uncle Fred (which would, of course, be my natural inclination). Instead, I was to ask questions like, "how much did it cost?" and "how many people are you expecting?"

As it turned out, Ken need not have worried. Jimmy Heineman (he asked me to call him Jimmy) met us at the door, and except for one sticky moment when he said, "So you're from California" to which I answered "well, Michigan really," he took control.

The exhibit was not completely set up yet, but it was mostly done. For those of you who went, you will remember that Jeeves greets you at the door, or actually a life-size cutout of Jeeves. Kenny took a picture of Jimmy and me standing next to it. Jimmy no doubt had visions of this picture, 8 x 10, on every door step in the Bay area. Smiling next to him, I knew it was destined for my scrapbook alone.

I got a brief autobiography of Mr. Heineman and how he came to be so interested in Wodehouse and amassed his vast collection. He gave me his phone number, as well as the name, address, and phone number of Bill Blood (telling me I should get in touch as he was organizing a society for Wodehouse). I used neither for fear of being unmasked as the impostor I was. Like Pongo who was instructed to tap his teeth with a pencil and smell of iodoform, we tried as much as possible to look like real newspaper people. Ken, of course, had the advantage over me that in that he was one, but I did my best, dropping the occasional journalistic expression and trying to act like something out of *The Front Page*.

It must have worked because we got the red-carpet treatment for sure. And soon I was too absorbed and enchanted to feel any guilt or discomfort.

I was shown the special case dedicated to the Empress of Blandings, the two cases on Jeeves and Bertie, the five doctoral theses on Wodehouse (three of which were in French), the case on imitators of

Wodehouse, the magazines, first editions, playbooks, sheet music, and on and on. I held in my hand the Complete Shakespeare that Wodehouse took with him into his internment and opened his diary to December 13, 1904 and read, "I set it down that I have arrived," when he had toted up his take as a writer and found it to be substantial. Jimmy and I did in fact discuss the fine points of various novels and stories. I gave him a copy of my thesis, "The Growth of Sweetness and Light," and he gave me a copy of the Wodehouse Centenary Book. He invited Kenny and me to the opening gala and the performance of Edward Duke's *Jeeves Takes Charge*, which we politely declined. The thing was, in a word, a love-feast.

It was a magical afternoon for me, and I always regretted that I did not take the plunge and stay for the opening. So what if sales in Cincinnati slipped? So what if Kenny and I were exposed? Would that have stopped Uncle Fred? Would it have stopped Psmith?

I received a very nice note from Jimmy shortly after our visit. I wanted so to write him and explain, but fear held my hand. I wanted to believe that Jimmy would be enough of a Wodehousean to appreciate the fact that we were impostors and why we did it, but I couldn't help thinking that most people are not pleased finding out that they have been had.

We did it out of fun and out of love, and, yes, there was a monetary gain (that book is quite valuable now), so it was a truly Wodehousean imposture. But was it wrong? Before you judge us for so deceiving this kind man, mark the sequel.

On June 26, 1998, I was seated in the fifth row at Sotheby's for the auction of the Heineman collection, prepared to purchase one or two lots of books to fill in my little collection. As the event was nearing the end, and I was quite done purchasing the few items I wanted and could afford, I was gripped with one of those mysterious urges one gets at auctions, and, impulsively—nay, uncontrollably, as if moved by some outside force—I raised my paddle. When the mists had cleared, I found myself the proud owner of lot 147, an eclectic collection of innumerable items whose description in the catalogue goes on for several pages and which arrived some weeks later in the form of five massive crates, each large enough to hold a grand piano. For the preceding seventeen years, I had thought back on that wonderful spring day in New York as a grand imposture in the style of Psmith, Uncle Fred, Jeff Miller, Mike Cardinal, and Packy Franklin. Staring at these huge boxes in my company's warehouse now, I felt more like Soapy Molloy, Oily Carlisle, and Smooth Sam Fisher—men too clever by half, whose impersonating machinations have come to naught and landed them deep in the mulligatawny. Oh, yes, my friends; Jimmy Heineman had gotten his revenge but good.

From the desk of E.
Detroit, MI
10 October, 2017

Only the Appetizer

It was the kind of August day mothers with toddlers pray for, so they can send the little monsters to the beach and down a Seconal to take a nap. The millennium was brand new, but the decade half gone. I'd just come down from Paso Robles, where the temperature was triple digits and the pinot noir grapes weren't just sun-kissed but gobsmacked, and, after inhaling a couple bottles the night before, what breeze I could find felt good against a head that felt full of igneous rocks. My morning coffee had at least partially lubricated my flannel tongue, and after a diner breakfast better imagined than described, I was almost prepared to start earning my keep, if you can call it that. I was staying at a dive in Westwood and was now making my way in a rented Caddy to UCLA, where I had to meet up with a gink named Armstrong who was taking a bunch of Midwestern yahoos on a nickel tour of Tinseltown. What I was doing with this busload of over-educated bozos is a story I'll save for a long winter night, assuming winter ever gets here.

The University campus is a city inside a city, and as good a microcosm of the burg that holds it as any, only with fewer suits and more hormones. Being summer, the locale was nearly barren, all the coeds baking on beaches somewhere, while the place was taken over by tourists and conventioneers. The little group I was supposed to join was here to celebrate the works of a scribbler called Wodehouse, who had done a stretch at Dulwich College, which made it old home week for me, as you could say I did some time there myself.

Armstrong was a straightforward, open-faced geek, and he greeted me warmly, almost like we'd been friends since the Stone Age. He was an actor, a tribe I usually avoid like the plague, and strictly B list to boot. I recognized him from his movies, of course, and was rather saddened to see him reduced to playing nursemaid to this bunch of clueless eggheads. We all loaded onto the bus, and it took us out Westwood Blvd to Wilshire, through the heart of Beverly Hills, so the yokels could rubberneck the hotties paying too much for too little on Rodeo Drive. Then we wound through West Hollywood, then East along Melrose, winding up at Paramount Studios for a wow finish. All the while, Armstrong's making like the guy from Hop On Hop Off, with a patter smooth as an ingénue on satin sheets, yapping away about Bogart and Bacall and Woody Allen and Loretta Young, mixing decades like a bartender mixing liquors for a Fuzzy Navel.

At Paramount, some studio geezer in designer jeans and cross trainers that had to cost a couple of dimes greets everyone and piles us into a screening room where we watch a five-minute promo for a new SciFi flick with a third-rate plot, second-rate star, and first-rate budget. And then we're done. I thought, "that's it?"

But it seems this was only the appetizer. The main course was on Saturday, when Armstrong was supposed to deliver thirty minutes straight dope on some book about a dentist. How he was going to make that interesting would be interesting in and of itself. It seems he'd delivered big time to a similar group of geezers a couple years ago, but since it was in Canada, everyone here had missed it. So the bimbo that organizes these gigs arranged for the next convention to be in his home town so she could rope him in where he can't duck out. Seems that was his MO when called on to speak at one of these shindigs. I heard these suckers were so afraid of getting behind the eight-ball a few years back, they even moved the whole shebang three months out of time just to keep Armstrong from ankling.

Well we all settled into the auditorium, and one slab of cheese after another sets his jaws flapping about Jeeves this and Mulliner that. But then this Armstrong comes out, and the gang really goes crazy with the clapping and hooting. Finally the dust settles, and he starts in. Well, I have to say, for a sawed-off little half-portion, he held them spell-bound from the very first sentence. I hadn't known Wodehouse at Dulwich—Plum, they called him—having just missed him by a summer holiday. But by the time Armstrong wrapped it up, I found myself kind of interested in the Old Boy and his take on this burg of ours, and the crazy, glitzy, cruel, sordid, beautiful business it enshrines, especially through the lens of this book, which, it turns out, isn't about a dentist at all.

Anyway, there was a lot more after that, but I lit out to meet a shamus I knew down in Inglewood. We were going to share a liquid lunch while he gave me the dope on another case I was working on.

Well, that was a dozen years ago, and now I get a call asking me to strong-arm this hambone into coughing up the MS of this talk to be included in a book. Seems there's money in his writing now, and someone wants to cash in. I took the gig. A job's a job. I only had to lean on him a little, and he folded like an old wallet. Hell, what a guy won't do for forty bucks a day plus expenses.

UNDER THE INFLUENCE
OF LAUGHING GAS

Curtis Armstrong

First given as a talk at The Wodehouse Society Convention in Hollywood, CA in 2005 and published in Plum Lines *in Spring 2006.*

Serial mayhem, drug use, alcoholism, alcohol and tobacco abuse by minors, violation of child-labor laws, child abandonment and endangerment, kidnapping, assault with a deadly weapon, juvenile delinquency, child-on-child violence, unwanted sexual contact.

Hollywood is responsible for much of what we see on television and in films. It is attacked like clockwork by the arbiters of public morals for corrupting American youth, inciting violence, diminishing attention spans, dumbing down our intellects, and encouraging the violent overthrow of our duly elected government—when we have one. Our seasonal earthquakes, floods, fires, and mudslides are considered a righteous judgment on a modern-day Cities of the Plain. As Wodehouse himself might put it, it's the kind of city that makes one wonder whether man is really God's last word. Let's face it, as far as many Americans are concerned, Hollywood might as well be France.

But the litany of violence and corruption I have listed above comes not from the latest hit series or erotic thriller, but from P. G. Wodehouse's 1936 novel *Laughing Gas*.

Ah, Hollywood, Hollywood! Bright city of sorrows, where fame deceives and temptation lurks, where souls are shriveled in the furnace of desire, whose streets are bathed with the shamed tears of betrayed maidens! Hollywood! Home of mean glories and spangled wretchedness, where the deathless fire burns for the outstretched wings of the guileless moth and beauty is broken on sin's cruel wheel.

Theodore Dreiser? No, it is P. G. Wodehouse, preeminent spreader of sweetness and light and—sometimes—hard-hitting commentator and trenchant social observer. Wodehouse's Hollywood stories and novels are rife with stark examples of an industry with a soul like something out of a Hogarth painting. It is not, I think, too much to claim that *Laughing Gas* does for show business what Upton Sinclair's *The Jungle* did for slaughterhouses. Sinclair's devastating exposé on conditions in the meatpacking industry caused a national scandal. *Laughing Gas* performs much the same function for the movie business, which has long given the phrase "meat processing" a whole new meaning.

It must be said that the public outrage to Wodehouse's revelations was considerably less vocal than it had been to Sinclair's. In fact, my research has revealed no public outrage at all. Nevertheless, *Laughing Gas* lays bare the Hollywood of the 1930s for all to see. As an outsider, Wodehouse saw behind the glamorous mask of Tinseltown, and this novel, unique in the Canon, reveals what lay behind that mask. And it wasn't pretty.

Consider this bleak monologue, a speech made even more horrifying when we realize that the words are coming out of a little boy's mouth—a little boy with golden ringlets:

> You betcher I'd strike a woman. Yessir, she'll get hers. And there's about six directors I'm going to poke in the snoot, and a whole raft of supervisors and production experts. And that press agent of mine. I'm going to poke him in the snoot, all right. Yessir! Matter of fact, you'd have a tough time finding someone I'm not going to poke in the snoot, once I'm big enough.

Truly, the resemblance between Joey Cooley and Russell Crowe is unmistakable.

The plight of child actors in Hollywood is well known, thanks to the widely publicized case of the young actor upon whom Joey

Cooley was based, right down to his initials: Jackie Coogan. Coogan, at one time the highest-paid child actor in the world, grew to man's estate ignorant of the fact that his mother had embezzled every cent he ever made. The resultant Jackie Coogan Law was enacted to protect young talent from being robbed blind by their nearest and dearest. Sadly, there were no watchdogs in place for young Joey Cooley or his peers. By the time we meet them in *Laughing Gas*, Wodehouse paints a grim and pitiful picture of Joey's predecessors at the top of the ladder: Tommy Murphy and Orlando Flower—former child stars thrown on Hollywood's ash heap once their usefulness has ended, leaving them to roam the mean streets of Beverly Hills like a pack of young coyotes, turning savagely on alpha male Joey in sequences that remind us of something out of a National Geographic special.

The truth is, Hollywood in the thirties glamorized its Temples, Coogans, and Cooleys publicly, while exploiting them ruthlessly behind the scenes. The public never saw Shirley Temple roused from bed at three o'clock in the morning to have her flaxen locks forced into hot curls. They were blissfully unaware of Judy Garland being force-fed diet pills by the studio to keep her weight down. But Wodehouse tips us off to all these abuses in *Laughing Gas*. Joey tells Reggie,

> Know what a serf is? ...I mean what's downtrodden and op-pressed and gets the dirty end of the stick all the time. That's me.... Shall I tell you something? ...I'm not allowed to play games, because I might get hurt. I'm not allowed to keep a dog, because it might bite me. I'm not allowed in the swimming pool because I might get drowned. And, listen, get this one. No candy, because I might put on weight.

A *cri de coeur* if ever we've heard one.

If there's one thing people can't get enough of these days, it is reading about the private peccadilloes, personal secrets, and hidden perversions of their favorite stars, and the more lurid and disgusting they are, the better they like them. As *Laughing Gas* shows, it was ever thus. But the increased appetite of today's public for the graphic de-tails of celebrities' private lives has had a predictable effect. Stars must now work especially hard at keeping their personal lives increasingly salacious just to keep up with market demand. Back in Wodehouse's day, alcoholism was a popular celebrity scandal of choice because it was something the average American could relate to. Indeed, alcohol abuse was so widespread during Hollywood's golden age that a cottage industry sprang up to support it. Everyone has seen the little kiosks that advertise Maps to Stars' Homes, but few realize that these were originally established to help intoxicated stars find their way back home after a night on the tiles. Domestic violence, drug addiction, bestiality, or pedophilia were less sympathetic failings, which just goes to show how far we've come.

In *Laughing Gas*, Wodehouse uses great subtlety in showing, even then, Hollywood's obsession with weight loss by substituting prunes for Benzedrine—Perfecto Prunes, to be precise. Joey Cooley is forced to eat them with every meal, as a diuretic, to keep his weight down. Then, to add insult to injury, the prunes are widely publicized in an early example of product placement. Of course, it could be argued that prunes were unlikely to be addictive, but that would have been cold comfort to Joey Cooley.

These days, you hear a lot of talk in Hollywood about the "fly-over." Some of you may not be familiar with this term. The fly-over is a Hollywood expression that refers to the whole of the continental United States, excluding New York and Los Angeles. In Wodehouse's day, it was called the sticks, the boonies, or God's Country. Joey Cooley hails from the heart of the fly-over: Chillicothe, Ohio, where hearts are pure and men are men, at least according to him. People in Hollywood have highly conflicted reactions to the fly-over. Joey's comment of "I don't care if Pittsburgh chokes. And that goes for Cincinnati, too" certainly reflects the opinion of many in Hollywood today—particularly those who were born and raised in places like Pittsburgh or Cincinnati and don't like to be reminded of it. At the same time, the importance of the fly-over to the bottom line in the industry is undeniable—hence Beulah Brinkwater's hiring of Eggy Mannering as an elocution coach to rid their star of his Ohio accent, which, she claims, "you could turn handsprings on." In other words, in Hollywood, it's okay to come from Ohio as long as you don't sound like you come from Ohio.

This rule of thumb remains true today: Some of you on the bus tour [during the Hollywood convention] may have noticed signs posted here and there that read, "Accent Elimination: Speak American like a Native"— which I don't think is technically what they mean to say, but it does show the degree to which people here tend to forget just how much country lies outside the cultural capitals of New York and Hollywood, if "cultural" is the word I'm looking for. Even Wodehouse has Ann Bannister arrange to take Joey back to his Ohio home "in a car," as if Chillicothe were down by the beach or something. Hollywood types are often accused of this kind of sunny geographical ignorance. In Christopher Guest's Hollywood satire *The Big Picture*, the studio executive, played by the late J. T. Walsh, asks the young would-be screenwriter where he comes from. "Chicago," the writer replies. "Oh," says the executive, "I have family in Ohio."

Wodehouse's geographical chops are a little suspect even as regards Hollywood and its environs. In *Laughing Gas*, he refers to "going down" to Malibu when he means "up." Likewise, in *Performing Flea*, he talks about going "down" to Santa Barbara, which is even further "up" than Malibu. But this sense of disorientation is common to people in my business. That's why chauffeured limousines were invented.

As for unwanted sexual contact, *Laughing Gas* delivers. Imagine the shame and humiliation a healthy young man would feel when he is told by an attractive young woman to take off his clothes at once because she wants to give him a bath. Okay, bad example. Imagine the shame and humiliation a healthy young man would feel when he is told that six hundred women from Michigan are lining up to kiss him, and he has to pretend to enjoy it. I understand that this sort of thing occurs even today in Hollywood, though God knows it's never happened to me, and I come from Michigan. Nevertheless, it's just this sort of behavior that gives everybody in town a black eye once the press gets hold of it. Let me just say right now that I've been in Hollywood for over twenty years, and I've never once been to a sex party or even been offered so much as a friendly threesome among friends.

And speaking of the press, its sinister machinations give *Laughing Gas* a critical plot point and gives us an interesting glimpse into Wodehouse's autobiography. Everyone is familiar with Wodehouse's ill-considered interview with Alma Whitaker of the *Los Angeles Times*, an interview that, according to Plum, resulted in his premature departure from Hollywood in 1931. *Laughing Gas*, written some five years later, replays this curious misstep in Wodehouse's life by introducing reporter Pomona Wycherly of the *Los Angeles Chronicle*.

You may recall that this Wycherly is at April June's house when Reggie Havershot, still in the body of Joey Cooley, narrowly escapes his tormentors, the former child-star thugs Murphy and Flower. Whycherly takes advantage of his breathless, rattled condition to get an interview, an interview made even more newsworthy by Joey's thoughtlessly smoking a much-needed cigarette and downing a purely medicinal snort or two. Reggie/Joey, pictured glass in hand, cigarette in mouth, is quoted as saying he's actually twenty-seven and prefers a pipe. All of this winds up on the front page of the Sunday edition, just as Wodehouse's interview did. The article effectively destroys the young actor's career in Hollywood, which is just fine by him, as it seems it was just fine for Wodehouse when it had happened to him.

But clear-eyed and razor sharp as Wodehouse's satire is throughout *Laughing Gas*, the sequence that tops them all is that which features April June's gang-for-hire: George, Eddie, and Fred. In a town clogged to the back teeth with hyphenates, these three stand alone: kidnapper-screenwriters. But as bad as kidnapping is, it's what they do to their victim once they have him under wraps that's truly monstrous: They pitch him a movie they're writing. I know what most people think when reading this part of the book: "Funny, yes, but that's a little much, isn't it?" Well, some ten years or so ago, a disc jockey here in Los Angeles sent one of his people to a corner in Beverly Hills at lunch time and had him stop people—completely at random—and ask them, "How is the screenplay coming?" Eight out of ten people had an answer.

Back in the thirties, when the Golden Age of Hollywood was cresting, and countless actors and playwrights from New York were surging west like some great race movement of the Middle Ages, a friend of playwright George S. Kaufman sent him a cable. This friend had already transplanted himself from New York to Hollywood and was writing to encourage his friend to do the same. "There are piles of gold in the streets, just waiting for you." Kaufman cabled back: "You mean I have to bend over and pick them up?"

Bending over and picking it up was pretty much how Wodehouse described his time in Hollywood. Of his work on *Rosalie*, he remarked, "No one wanted me to hurry. When it was finished, they thanked me politely and remarked that as musicals didn't seem to be going so well, they guessed they would not use it. That about sums up what I was called upon to do for my $104,000. Isn't it amazing?"

And to Townend he wrote, "I am sort of an Ogre to movie studios now...I don't care personally, as I don't think I could do picture writing. It needs a definitely unoriginal mind." Plum took considerable pride in claiming he did so little work he had time "to write a novel, and nine short stories, besides brushing up my golf, getting an attractive sun-tan and perfecting my Australian crawl."

In *Wodehouse: A Life*, Robert McCrum claims Wodehouse mythologized his year in Hollywood, particularly his exit from it. Plum's self-mythologizing looms large in McCrum's book, but in this case, I think he's mistaken. What strikes me as so interesting about Wodehouse's account of his exile from Tinseltown is how similar it is to his account of his exile from the Hong Kong and Shanghai Bank so many years before. You all remember that one: The Pirandelloesque short story written on the blank page of the new ledger about the opening of the new ledger, the page then torn out, the subsequent discovery by the office manager, who had it in for the stationer; the office uproar, the beleaguered stationer claiming only an idiot would tear a page out of a new ledger, have you an idiot working for you? The manager saying, "Well, we do have P. G. Wodehouse." Poor Plum called onto the carpet and grilled and finally coming clean, the nibs forming a hollow square and drumming him out of finance forever. Now that's mythologizing. What's really amazing about life in Hollywood is how hard it is to mythologize something that is so unreal to begin with.

From the desk of E.
Detroit, MI
23 October, 2017

Virtually Vibrating with Pride

Convention followed convention in its predictable biennial way, but Curtis did not make it to Providence in 2007 nor to St. Paul in 2009. By now, The Pickering Motor Company (as the Detroit chapter of TWS is called) had expanded quite a bit beyond the original group of close friends who rallied round to help me put on the 2003 convention, and the newer members were tired of hearing the oldsters reminisce about those days. So we put in a bid for the 2011 convention and were awarded the contract. Once again in charge of the speakers program, once again I turned to my old friend and imposed upon him to join in the fun.

Whilst in 2003 it was necessary for me to move the convention from October (Curtis's busy season) to August, when actors rest in sleepy summer, such a move was highly impolitic eight years later. For one thing, the Toronto convention had the lowest attendance of any TWS convention in history, and, for another, the newer Pickerings insisted that the Saturday banquet take place on Wodehouse's birthday. We even named the convention "Happy 130th Birthday, Plum." When I reached out to Curtis, knowing it was unlikely he would relent, he shockingly replied that he would be there with his hair in braid and even jumped at the chance to speak again. Clearly, he was now at ease in his role as Wodehouse scholar and had gotten it thoroughly up his nose.

Having wrung all there was from Wodehouse's Hollywood, Curtis now turned his attention to other aspects of the Canon. He informed me of the name of his talk but refused to tell me what it was about. In our correspondence, he did communicate from time to time that he was "having difficulty" with it, but around three months before coming to Dearborn, he let me know that all was well, and he was quite happy with it. "I don't think it's as funny as the other two," he wrote, "but I do think it will hold up."

It is hard for me to comment on its "funniness" as I was rather distracted when he actually gave the talk. We had a number of technical issues that morning, and I was in charge of keeping the program moving along. Our first speaker went about twenty minutes over, and I was in a blind panic about whether we would finish in time for lunch. Also, I had yet to give my own speech—a multi-media presentation that called for the most perfect timing—and was worried about that. And finally, Curtis's father showed up to see his son's talk, and I was sitting with him and paying more attention to him than I was to Curtis. You would have thought by this time that the old fellow was used to seeing his son performing on a stage or in a film, and that performances like his in *Revenge of the Nerds*, *Ray*, and *Akeela and the Bee* would have made him think of something like a lecture at a Wodehouse convention as rather a low-level affair. But, on my honor, the honest fellow was virtually vibrating with pride watching his son deliver this talk, a grin spread across his face that would have lit up Times Square.

The long and short of it is that I actually have no remembrance of how the talk went over and whether people found it humorous or not. In fact, I didn't even really hear a word of it myself, as I was watching the clock and his father and noting the hotel manager at the back of the room tapping his foot and pointing to his watch.

So it was such a pleasure for me to read it when it was printed in *Plum Lines* and truly appreciate how insightful and polished it is. "Hold up" is not the *mot juste* for this work. It is a true piece of Wodehouse scholarship. Perhaps it is because I do not remember the talk as given that it strikes me as more of a written piece than a speech. In everything Curtis has written—from his letters to me to his recently published memoir, *Revenge of the Nerd* (available at Amazon.com and fine bookstores everywhere)—I can hear Curtis's voice, so this is normally a distinction I do not make. But this piece has a certain formality to it that the other talks do not.

It was courageous of Curtis to approach Wodehouse's writing from this angle. As he points out, it is not the direction from which the reader typically comes. And there is always the trap of getting a little too serious—something definitely to be avoided in writing about Wodehouse, as Alexander Cockburn relates in *Homage to P. G. Wodehouse*:

High seriousness about [Wodehouse] brings to mind poor Professor Scully [and his] attempt in 1902 to describe a smile scientifically...Scully doggedly dissected "the drawing back and slight lifting of the corners of the mouth, which partially uncover the teeth, the curving of the naso-labial furrows..."

Wodehouse is peculiarly resistant to what we might term the naso-labial approach, which is possibly why critics have had such a hard time with him.

Despite the subject matter, Curtis brilliantly avoids naso-labilia.

There is also the temptation, when getting political, to try to find some deeper meaning in his work. Wodehouse himself has warned critics not to do so, writing in *Over Seventy*,

[I have no] particular message for humanity. I am still plugging away and not the ghost of one so far, so it begins to look as though, unless I suddenly hit mid-season form in my eighties, humanity will remain a message short.

Curtis cleverly avoids this trap as well.

Re-reading it again now, after having read his recently published memoirs, I notice that it follows the same pattern: it begins with a humorous review, covers a number of interesting and revelatory points, and ends with a poignant reflection. In a sense, Curtis seems to be presenting Wodehouse's struggle with his changing world in the same way that he, Curtis, presented his own struggle with changes in our world and his profession. Maybe I am reading more into this, having read his book and this paper in such close succession. But I don't think so. At the very least, it amply justifies his father's response.

WODEHOUSE
IN A CHANGING WORLD

Curtis Armstrong

First given as a talk at The Wodehouse Society Convention in Dearborn, MI in 2011 and published in Plum Lines *in Summer 2011.*

P. G. Wodehouse has been called many things, but mysterious isn't one of them. He was a simple man, in the very best meaning of the phrase, whose life centered around his work, who savored cricket and soap operas, and who enjoyed a couple of quick ones in the gloaming. One real mystery, at least according to some, is how Wodehouse managed to live and write through two world wars, the Great Depression, an internment by the Nazis, the death of his daughter, the Cold War, the Atomic Age, and the turmoil of the 1960s and early seventies, and yet could consistently create characters who remain untouched and apparently ignorant of what is happening in the world.

But the truth is, Wodehouse's characters did not pass through these tempests completely unscathed. People assume that the only disruption in the serene flow of Bertie's life is when he's forbidden access to Anatole's dinners or when he's engaged to be married to Madeline Bassett again. Well, as far as Bertie is concerned, that's true, but there is a more serious offstage thunder rumbling on the very first page of *The Inimitable Jeeves*:

> "How is the weather, Jeeves?"
> "Exceptionally clement, sir."
> "Anything in the papers?"

"Some slight friction threatening in the Balkans, sir. Otherwise, nothing."

It's true that Bertie doesn't express much in the way of concern about friction in the Balkans—in fact, he responds to this news with a question about putting his shirt on Privateer at the two o'clock. After all, Bertie and Jeeves lived in a world without a twenty-four-hour news cycle. There is no television over the bar at the Drones Club, and if there were, it would more likely be tuned to test matches than CNN. But this doesn't mean the stories are void of political event. Political meetings could descend into vulgar brawling, but so too could prize-giving ceremonies and the occasional clean, bright entertainment. In general, though, politics tend to be avoided except in the noble aid of a joke, which is not a bad idea when you think about the state of politics these days. If conservative politicians tend to predominate in the stories, it's just because they seem funnier when, for example, they are trapped on the roofs of summerhouses after being chivvied about by mad swans. It just seems people like that have more to lose. A. B. Filmer, the conservative cabinet minister from "Jeeves and the Impending Doom," is a great example, as is Sir Raymond Bastable from *Cocktail Time*. The examples are legion.

As a rule, class-bound people in Wodehouse who don't drink, don't smoke, don't gamble, have a lot of money and power, and have no sense of humor are just asking for it. They are always the ones putting up barricades in the path of true love. They insist on standing for the Conservative seat at Bottleton East, or somewhere, but at the same time, they're the ones who have to worry about their youthful indiscretions coming to light in some old reprobate's memoirs. Men who resemble a cartoon of Capital from a communist newspaper exist not to make political points, but to deny their nephews enough money to open onion soup bars in Piccadilly Circus or marry an impecunious chorus girl. The Marx Brothers understood the value of knocking the self-important off their pedestals and then destroying the pedestals while they're at it. And so, on occasion, did P. G. Wodehouse.

Jeeves's awareness of friction threatening in the Balkans is just one example of the real world imposing upon the land of eternal summer that is Wodehouse's fictional world. But politicians, like headmasters,

aunts, and bishops, are basically stock characters in the Wodehouse
Canon and can be pretty much taken as read. So for our purposes, I
will focus on the social or political movements that actually intruded
on the lives of Wodehouse's characters: socialism and fascism. And
how even these disruptions, like a summer shower at Blandings, pass
quickly, leaving not a wrack behind.

We'll begin with fascism because, of the two movements, it seems
to be of the least immediate concern to Wodehouse's characters. In
their changing world, the human (or nearly human) face of British fascism was, of course, Roderick Spode, later Lord Sidcup. The introduction of Spode shows that Wodehouse's treatment of comic right-wing
extremism differs from his depiction of left-wing extremism. Spode
is the only memorable character in the stories to represent fascism.
While we hear of the Black Shorts, we never see them, and by the
time Spode is knighted, he has disbanded his followers. The socialists,
however, have no such single figurehead of the movement. There are
certainly memorable characters, but no national figurehead like Spode.
The other difference is that Spode fills his role as the evil nemesis
without ever talking about the glories of his political beliefs, while the
socialists, whether en masse or in a cozy *tête-à-tête* around the tea table,
seem to do little else.

Spode bestrides Wooster's world like a Colossus, but his reputation
as a charismatic fascist chieftain seems, on the surface, unwarranted.
Spode is a thug. You can dress him up, but you can't take him anywhere. It is easier to imagine him kicking out shop windows or lay-
ing into striking picketers with a wooden club than as the leader and
mastermind of a political movement. And it is Bertie Wooster, of all
people, who sees Spode clearly and sees him whole. "Stirring" is not a
word that normally comes to mind when we think of Bertie Wooster,
but stirring is what his memorable condemnation of Spode and his
politics comes closest to being:

> "It is about time," I proceeded, "that some public-spirited per-
> son came along and told you where you got off. The trouble
> with you, Spode, is that just because you have succeeded in
> inducing a handful of half-wits to disfigure the London scene
> by going about in black shorts, you think you're someone. You

hear them shouting 'Heil, Spode!' and you imagine it is the Voice of the People. That is where you make your bloomer. What the Voice of the People is saying is, 'Look at that frightful ass Spode swanking about in footer bags! Did you ever in your puff see such a perfect perisher?'"

Add a Max Steiner score in the background, and it could almost be Victor Laszlo in *Casablanca*.

There is no better example than Spode of the old adage about living by the sword. His fear of being exposed as a closeted designer of ladies' undergarments is only one of his problems. In addition to being hit in the eye with a potato at a political rally, which sort of goes with the territory, this amateur dictator has been knocked unconscious once by Bertie's Aunt Dahlia, once by a cook, and once by a curate. In *The Code of the Woosters*, Gussie Fink-Nottle wallops him over the head with an oil painting, after which Bertie wraps him in a sheet, breaks a china vase over his head, and puts out a cigarette on his hand. By themselves, any one of these unfortunate occurrences could be overlooked, but put them together, and they spell a public relations disaster. When word gets out to the other fascists that you can't get the upper hand of a newt-collecting freak like Gussie Fink-Nottle, you can start considering your days as a Man of Destiny officially numbered.

Despite these setbacks, Spode is such an overwhelming personality that it's easy to forget that fascism is addressed elsewhere in Wodehouse's writings. One example occurs in the Mr. Mulliner story "Buried Treasure":

> The situation in Germany had come up for discussion in the bar parlour of the Angler's Rest, and it was generally agreed that Hitler was standing at the crossroads and would soon be compelled to do something definite. His present policy, said a Whisky and Splash, was mere shilly-shallying.
>
> "He'll have to let it grow or shave it off," said the Whisky and Splash. "He can't go on sitting on the fence like this. Either a man has a moustache or he has not. There can be no middle course."

Here, two paragraphs manage to satirize both Hitler and the genial topers of the Angler's Rest, whose awareness of the Nazi menace apparently begins and ends with a discussion of the Fuhrer's moustache.

As we move from fascism to socialism, we find Wodehouse working with a wider, richer palette. Appropriately for a movement that appealed to the masses, he no longer restricts himself to a single character, but expands to small groups or even mobs. He would appear to have as little sympathy for the socialists as he does their counterparts on the right, though it must be said that the attributes he assigns to the various socialists in the stories range from dullness to monomania to drunkenness to teetotalling (just as bad) to sociopathy, and, finally, to murderousness. Worse still, one of them has no roof to his mouth, always a red flag in Wodehouse's world.

In "Archibald and the Masses," the subject of socialism is raised by a Pint of Bitter and a Light Lager at that hotbed of political disputation, the Angler's Rest:

> "This here Socialism," said a Pint of Bitter thoughtfully. "You see a lot of that about nowadays. Seems to be all the go."
>
> "Spreading all the time, Socialism is [said a Light Lager]. May be something in it, too. What I mean, it doesn't hardly seem right somehow that you and I should be living off the fat of the land, as the saying is, while there's others, in humbler circumstances, who don't know where to turn for their next half-pint."

Archibald Mulliner, in pursuit of love, as usual, hears the siren call of socialism. He has a valet, Meadowes, who is a member of the League for the Dawn of Freedom, whose object is, he informs his employer, to hasten the coming revolution. Archibald takes a hard line with his man: "Now, listen, Meadowes," said Archibald firmly. "Fun's fun, but no rot about stabbing me with a dripping knife. I won't have it, do you understand?"

Archibald's attempts to cluster round the masses are predictably catastrophic, but don't really have anything to do with socialism, per se—more a series of simple misunderstandings which Archibald could look back on and laugh about once he was released. No, to really see the effects of socialism on Wodehouse's world, we must go to the Wooster and Psmith chronicles.

Bertie's first recorded brushes with the socialist revolution occur through the good offices of his friend Bingo Little. In *The Inimitable Jeeves*, Bingo, falling in and out of love not wisely but often, plays Virgil to Bertie's Dante, guiding him through numerous circles of romantic hell, starting in a blighted tea and bun shop near Piccadilly and ending with marriage to the prominent romance novelist Rosie M. Banks.

In the middle of this snipe-like search for love, Bertie is introduced to the most recent love of Bingo's life, Charlotte Corday Rowbotham, along with her father, Comrade Rowbotham, and the rival for Charlotte's affections, Comrade Butt. It is probably not a coincidence that Wodehouse invents surnames for his socialists in this story that both manage to suggest the human posterior. The three are members in good standing of the Heralds of the Red Dawn, which Bingo has joined in order to pursue his wooing. Old Rowbotham is described by Bingo as "A delightful chap. Wants to massacre the bourgeoisie, sack Park Lane and disembowel the hereditary aristocracy. Well, nothing could be fairer than that, what?" This tale of love and socialism features two scenes in which the Red Dawn's most stirring orators—Comrade Butt and Bingo in a fake beaver—work up an appreciative crowd, but the only physical violence occurs when Comrade Butt exposes Bingo by debearding him, and Bingo grabs Butt by the neck and tries to twist his head off.

Say what you will about Spode, he never actually tried to kill Bertie with a knife and then burn his house down. Brinkley, Jeeves's temporary replacement in *Thank You, Jeeves*, does both. Another firm subscriber to the rivers-of-aristocratic-blood theory of solving the workers' problems, Brinkley returns to Bertie's cottage after a night on the tiles and decides to say it with carving knives. Bertie recalled him as being "quite thin when I knew him, and very gloomy, you might say sinister. Always seemed to be brooding on the coming revolution when he would be at liberty to chase me down Park Lane with a dripping knife." Brinkley is an unusual case, though. When we next encounter him in *Much Obliged, Jeeves*, he has changed his name, his waistline, and his politics. Having come into a sizable fortune, Bingley, as he is now known, reappears as a kind of conservative captive balloon, and as obnoxious as ever. Jeeves is uncharacteristically blunt when he says, "I disapprove of Bingley. He is dishonest. Not a man to be trusted."

Wodehouse's most famous socialist is, of course, Rupert Psmith, though his orthodoxy is questionable. "I've just become a Socialist," Psmith tells Mike Jackson moments into their friendship. "It's a great scheme. You ought to be one. You work for the equal distribution of property, and start by collaring all you can and sitting on it."

But apart from using it as an excuse for bagging Spiller's sitting room, socialism doesn't seem to figure largely in Psmith's life, save as an amusing fashion accessory, sort of like the way I cheerfully affected a walking stick during my college years. "Others are content to talk about redistribution of wealth," he says, sounding a little like Ukridge. "I go out and do it."

Socialism gets its grandest treatment in *Psmith in the City*. In this slender novel, Wodehouse devotes nothing fewer than three full chapters to Mike and Psmith's adventures in socialism. Psmith is delighted to discover his and Mike's supervisor, Waller, is a staunch socialist, coincidentally making him one of the few characters in the Psmith saga who actually deserves the appellation "Comrade." By mid-story, they are invited to come to hear Waller speak on Sunday at Clapham Common, with supper at Waller's home afterward.

Guided to the speaker's platform by Waller, the two are just in time to hear two of Waller's associates, Comrades Wotherspoon and Prebble, addressing the masses. Here we can do no better than let the author describe the scene:

> Comrade Wotherspoon was a tall, thin man with side-whiskers and a high voice. He scattered his aitches as a fountain its sprays in a strong wind. He was very earnest. Comrade Prebble was earnest, too. Perhaps even more so than Comrade Wotherspoon. He was handicapped to some extent, however, by not having a palate. This gave to his profoundest thoughts a certain weirdness, as if they had been uttered in an unknown tongue. The crowd was thickest around his platform. The grown-up section plainly regarded him as a comedian, pure and simple, and roared with happy laughter when he urged them to march

upon Park Lane and loot the same without mercy or scruple. The children were more doubtful. Several had broken down, and been led away in tears.

It may have been a different time, or it could just be the difference between Hyde Park and Clapham Common, but once Waller goes from the usual red-meat subject of socialism to his other pet passion, temperance, the response of the crowd couldn't be more different than that which Bertie experienced in *The Inimitable Jeeves*. The crowd turns into an ugly mob, and our heroes barely escape in one piece.

Dinner at the Waller residence following this debacle is even worse, if only because Mike and Psmith cannot, out of common courtesy, fight their way out of it. An awkward, dismal affair deteriorates into a lovers' quarrel between Waller's daughter and her fiancé over the subject of women's suffrage. "That fatal topic," murmurs Psmith, who was probably also aware of friction threatening in the Balkans.

Change in the world of Wodehouse, though, doesn't necessarily have to be of the epoch-defining variety, and some stories, while sticking to the traditional forms and characters, bear every hallmark of having been written in a changed world. "Bingo Bans the Bomb" is a story which could only have been written during the nuclear disarmament protests of the sixties, and if you don't believe me, get a load of the Pan paperback edition of *Plum Pie*, featuring the Hon. Mabel Murgatroyd in a cleavage-revealing polka dot romper.

In *Cocktail Time*, Wodehouse's foray into long-form satire, Sir Raymond Bastable becomes so outraged when his hat is knocked off with a Brazil nut fired from the smoking room of the Drones Club that he writes a scathing novel on the subject of the current Lost Generation. The book becomes a *cause célèbre*, turning the pseudonymous author into a kind of cross between Henry Miller and Kingsley Amis. Sex, Wodehouse tells us, had crept into the narrative in rather large quantities. While Wodehouse spares us the details, the book was daring enough to be railed against from pulpits and condemned in editorials across the country. Even the cover illustration pulled no punches, depicting, as Wodehouse puts it, "a young man with a monocle in his right eye doing the rock 'n' roll with a young woman in her step-ins."

It's remarkable to realize that Wodehouse's work appeared regularly throughout every upheaval, war, and social or political change in the first three-quarters of the twentieth century. Perhaps even more remarkable is that, throughout that time and ever since, he has continued, through the timeless richness of his humor, to bring a moment of escape to people the world over, people who face a changing world as terrifying as any in Wodehouse's lifetime. Certainly, social change and political upheaval were not unknown to Wodehouse's fictional world. They were just seen through the same genially warped looking glass as anything else there.

When the Nazis swept into Wodehouse's idyllic garden at Le Touquet, it was a "real world" incursion of the most unforgiving kind. Wodehouse was told that he had ten minutes to pack before being sent off to an internment camp. It is telling that the only book he took with him was the complete works of Shakespeare. Not Agatha Christie or Erie Stanley Gardner. Shakespeare. I suspect he knew he was facing a frightening future and reached for a book that would sustain him, cheer him: a book by a writer who could take him out of the nightmare reality in which he found himself, who could bring light to the darkness that surrounded him.

I am, of course, not comparing Wodehouse to Shakespeare, which would be unfair to Shakespeare. But in a world in which it sometimes seems that the Spodes are always winning, I recommend a similar palliative. Turn often to the works of P. G. Wodehouse.

From the desk of C.
Los Angeles, CA
6 November, 2017

Brightest Lights and Rarest Wits

Even after I had first been published in *Plum Lines*; even after I had made my first, tentative forays into organized Wodehouse fandom, if "organized" is the word I'm looking for; even after delivering my first couple of papers to patient and generous attendees at Society meetings in Toronto, Los Angeles and Detroit; I say, even after all that, when it would appear there were no more mountains to scale, no more experiences to enjoy, no other bucket on my list, there was one regular event in the world of Wodehouse in which I considered myself unworthy of participation, and that was the P G Wodehouse Society (UK) Biennial Formal Dinner.

It takes nothing away from the extraordinary events staged for the Wodehouse faithful in the U.S., Europe, and elsewhere when I say that there was something about the Formal Dinner that intimidated me. I had seen pictures. I had read the papers lightly disguised as "toasts" delivered to those distinguished members. I had seen candid photos of American members like Elliott chatting easily with Norman Murphy or Tony Ring, hobnobbing with the Duke of Kent or Sir Edward Cazalet, or, most especially, his daughter, the actress Lara Cazalet (on whom I had developed a long-distance crush); I saw all of them rosy of countenance, holding lovely, long-stemmed glasses filled with what was obviously champagne of the finest vintage. I knew that such things were possible, such an Elysium achievable. And yet, my native shyness, my colonial sense of inadequacy, my deep-bred American fear of using the wrong fork, or asking for a glass of hock with the meat course, held me back.

Elliott, though, suffered from none of these insecurities. Every two years, he'd fly over to London, don the soup-and-fish, and blandly mingle with his betters, bantering genially with the Wodehouse World's brightest lights and rarest wits. I could just imagine him, holding forth on some arcane piece of Wodehouseana to an enthralled group of scholars beneath the blackened oak beams soaring above them and under the very eyes, as it were, of Charles the Second, frowning down from his perch on the wall. I would always say, "Next time! Definitely next time," and I would say it so fervently, I almost believed it myself.

Finally, throwing my unmanly trepidation aside, I did attend my first Biennial Formal Dinner, but it took me until October of 2016 to do so, and I only did it then because my daughter Lily, then living in London, was invited too, and we had both been asked to participate in the Dinner's Clean, Bright Entertainment—a tradition with the U.K. society—along with, among other luminaries, HRH The Duke of Kent and my fantasy Biennial Dinner companion, Lara Cazalet. And it was all just as glorious as I had imagined.

But as confident, I'll say even as *soignée,* as Elliott had been in the years during which he was a respected regular at these gatherings, there was one invitation extended to him that chilled even his nerves of steel: when he was asked, as a last-minute replacement, to deliver the all-important Toast to Wodehouse and the Society; it was an awesome responsibility under any circumstances, but even more so when Elliott realized he would the first American ever to have done so.

Such was his concern that he actually called me in to give the toast a critical once-over, but even in its roughest form, it was clear to me that there was no need for concern. That he should've, on such short notice, delivered the following piece was and remains a source of amazement to me. His address combined the very best of classic Wodehouse scholarship with self-deprecating humor and the honest love of a true aficionado.

The stage is set, then, in the cloistered, venerable hall of Gray's Inn, London, October 2010, as Elliott Milstein, former President of The Wodehouse Society (US), steps up to the podium...

A TOAST TO P. G. WODEHOUSE
AND TO THE P G WODEHOUSE SOCIETY

Elliott Milstein

This toast was delivered in October 2010 in London, England.

When addressing a group of Wodehouseans in a formal setting like this, it is pretty much *de rigueur* to begin by making some reference to the prize-giving scene from *Right Ho, Jeeves*. And though I am, at the moment, easily as well-sozzled as Gussie Fink-Nottle was on that notable occasion, I will demur.

You see, as I prepared this little talk, I was more reminded of Woody Allen at the 2002 Academy Awards when he was asked to introduce an homage of his beloved New York City. He said that he told the organizers of the Oscars,

> "God, you can do much better than me, you know, why not get Martin Scorsese or Mike Nichols or Spike Lee or Sidney Lumet," I kept naming names, you know, and said, "look, I've given you fifteen names of guys who are more talented than I am, and smarter and classier," and they said, "yes, but they were not available."

And so it was with me when I opened an email from Tony Ring last month, requesting my participation tonight after the original speaker had dropped out. They hemmed, he said, and hawed and searched their vast databases—which I took to be the polite British way of saying "scraped the bottom of the barrel"—and found me. I must admit, I was a tad miffed at being an also-ran, but after being informed that speakers at these wonderful dinners are not asked to pay the price of admission, I jumped at the opportunity. It's the American in me.

Of course, it's a little hard on all of *you*. Here you are, on this night of nights, The P G Wodehouse Society (UK) Formal Dinner, and rather than being treated to the wit and wisdom of some home-grown luminary like, say, Stephen Fry, speaking in the dulcet tones of the Queen's own, you are subjected to the monotonous nasal whine of an obscure Midwesterner. And if that's not asking for bread and being handed a stone, I don't know what is.

And yet, it is rather *à propos* when you reflect that Wodehouse himself lived more years among us Yanks than he ever did on this scepter'd isle, ultimately becoming an American citizen. Consider, too, that one of his autobiographical works was entitled *America, I Like You*. And he had reason to like us. America was, after all, the making of his career, having visited us in 1904 when, he says, his "income rose like a rocketing pheasant."

Also, while for most people the term "The World of Wodehouse" conjures up Blandings Castle, Brinkley Manor, and Berkeley Square, many of Wodehouse's stories and novels take place in New York, Long Island, and the bizarro world of Hollywood, or as he liked to call it, "Dottyville-on-the-Pacific." It is true that he rarely wrote about or graced the great fly-over, as we in the Midwest are so enchantingly referred to by our coast-hugging brethren, but what of that? We don't hold that against him. Across the plains and mountains of our great land, chapters of the American Wodehouse Society have broken out like an eczema.

That being said, I must admit that Wodehouse is not as much in the forefront of the American consciousness as he is here. For instance, while many American news outlets recently mentioned that our latest Supreme Court is historic in that it includes three women for the first time, it is the British media that pointed out that it includes three Wodehouseans. (Although that may not be an historic event; for all we know, Louis Brandeis and Oliver Wendell Holmes frequently discussed their favorite Mulliner stories while Hugo Black pelted them with bread rolls.)

The problem is that Wodehouse aficionados are somewhat thinner on the ground in America than here. Not that we don't have many—the U.S. Wodehouse Society now numbers well over a thousand members—but we have so much more ground to cover. In America, one often has to travel vast distances to find a fellow Wodehousean. I, for one, live in a Wodehouse wilderness, so instead of enjoying frequent meetings and events like those this Society boasts, I have to endure my friends and neighbors constantly asking me, "What, exactly, is the attraction of this Wodehouse guy, anyway?"

On such occasions I could, of course, simply say that he is funny, but if they don't get that on their own, what's the use? And, of course, it is so much more than that. I could point out, for instance, how vivid and memorable his characters are, like Bertie and Jeeves, who are now so famous that when referred to in general discourse, no explanation of them or their creator is required; or how the Wodehouse world is so brilliantly drawn, it has become part of the Anglo-American literary landscape; or how the plots of his best novels have more twists and turns than a one-armed contortionist with hives.

But for me, the great joy of reading Wodehouse is the language, the craftsmanship of the writing itself. We laugh, we enjoy the goofy characters, we immerse ourselves in the world, but what gets *me* is just how darn good the writing is.

Of course, there are the nifties—those amazing little one-liners like "Jeeves lugged my purple socks out of the drawer as if he were a vegetarian fishing a caterpillar out of his salad"; or "The Duke shot back in his chair, and his moustache, foaming upwards as if a gale had struck it, broke like a wave on the stern and rockbound coast of the Dunstable nose"; or, my father's favorite, "if ever he had seen a fermenting aunt, this fermenting aunt was that fermenting aunt."

But I find the true genius of his writing emerges in more extensive passages. I could give any of a thousand examples, but one that always sticks in my mind is the flowerpot scene in *Leave it to Psmith*, all of which is just brilliant, but especially the moment when Lord Emsworth is awakened by Baxter's hurling flowerpots through the window. Several flowerpots have already come crashing into his room, but he is only aroused finally by one that hits him as he lies in bed. The scene continues:

> He looked at the flower-pot. It had no message for him. He had not put it there. He never took flower-pots to bed. Once, as a child, he had taken a dead pet rabbit, but never a flower-pot. The whole affair was completely inscrutable; and his lordship, unable to solve the mystery, was on the point of taking the statesmanlike course of going to sleep again, when something large and solid whizzed through the open window and crashed against the wall, where it broke, but not into such small fragments that he could not perceive that in its prime it, too, had been a flower-pot.

That last sentence is certainly one of the finest ever penned in the English language, and all the more brilliant in its setup with a series of short, simple declarative statements. And, of course, it is screamingly funny.

While working on my Wodehouse thesis at the University of Toronto, one day, in the St Mike's library, I was confronted by a professor with the accusation that it was a waste of academic effort to study a writer whose entire output had no redeeming feature but merely that it was funny. It was the word "merely" that made the iron enter into my soul. So it was with me the work of a moment to hop up to the third floor, take *Plum Pie* from the shelf, photocopy the final chapter—an essay entitled "A Note on Humor"—and hand it to him, pointing to this paragraph:

> I think we should all be sorry for humorists and try to be kind to them, for they are so vulnerable. You can blot the sunshine from their lives in an instant by telling them you don't see what's funny in *that,* and if there is something funny in it, you can take all the heart out of them by calling them facetious or describing them as "mere humorists." A humorist who is called mere not only winces. He frets. He mopes. He refuses to eat his cereal. He goes about with his hands in his pockets and his lower lip jutting out, kicking stones and telling himself that the lot of a humorist is something that ought not to happen

to a dog, and probably winds up by going in for "sick" humor, like Lenny Bruce, and the trouble about being like Lenny Bruce is that the cops are always arresting you, which must cut into your time rather annoyingly.

I took it as a personal victory that the next day in class, he read a section of the essay out loud, which would have been a highly edifying experience for my fellow students had he not broken out laughing so hard and so frequently as to be completely incomprehensible. While he would still not admit that Wodehouse was deserving of serious study, after that performance, he had to acknowledge not just Wodehouse's incredible talent, but also the value of his humor.

And humor is more valuable now than ever. We live in a world where quotidian calamities assault us on all sides: the international situation is as dire as any we have ever faced, starvation and oppression run rampant from Africa to Asia, the underpinning of the world economy is on the shakiest of grounds, and government officials, from Washington to Whitehall, seem to be comprised entirely of either Baxters and Spodes or the less IQ-endowed members of the Drones Club. What better way to stiffen the sinews against the day than to pick up a Wodehouse, open it at random, and read something like, "she resembled a Ziegfeld Follies girl who had been left out in the rain and swollen a bit"?

So, therefore, I invite you all to lift your glasses to toast one who has brought so much joy to so many, a humorist no one dares call "mere," the Master of the English Language, and the finest writer of either side of the Atlantic, the late Sir Pelham Grenville Wodehouse and to The P G Wodehouse Society (UK) that triumphantly carries on the noble cause of spreading sweetness and light.

From the desk of C.
Los Angeles, CA
15 November, 2017

Young Anglophiles with Wildly Eccentric Tastes

I have a special affection for this piece, both for its scholarship and for its subject.

The theme is friendship, and friendship, after all, is what inspired this project from the first. Elliott and I have talked about how Wodehouse essentially introduced the two of us to begin with. But it is remarkable when I think how central Wodehouse was to our relationship in the early years.

My mother is now well into her eighties, and her memory is rapidly failing, but when I mention Elliott's name, she never fails to recall standing in the kitchen while listening to the two of us in the living-room, reading Wodehouse out loud, and roaring with laughter. She remembers nothing else about my closest friend in high school, but that memory stayed with her.

Strangely, I have no recollection of this event at all, but that's possibly because there were just too many others like it. While in this case my memory of sharing Wodehouse with Elliott has come to me second hand, there were many others that I have no difficulty recalling. In our high school years, and then beyond, we were still in many cases reading Wodehouse books for the first time. So whether we were in my house in Berkley, his family's house in Warren, MI or Kingsville, Ont., his rooms at college in Toronto, my parents' house in London, or anywhere else, recent discoveries of new favorites were being read aloud, often with brandies and pipes to hand, as befitted a couple of young Anglophiles with what must have been regarded by our other Detroit friends as wildly eccentric tastes.

As Elliott points out, when Bertie Wooster referred to his friends, he could set a dramatically high rhetorical bar: Damon and Pythias. Indeed, almost every time he makes reference to close or old friends, it is with the kind of exquisite hyperbole that naturally has the effect of keeping any actual human connection from getting in the way of the jokes.

While I suppose there's nothing wrong with shooting for the Pythagorean ideal in friendships, in the real world, some of the most enduring and long lasting can find their roots in something a little humbler, like a mutual love of Pelham Grenville Wodehouse.

WHO IS BERTIE'S "BFF"?

Elliott Milstein

This article was first published in Plum Lines *in Spring 2009.*

I have long enjoyed the delightful ambiguity of the expression, "A friend in need is a friend indeed." When younger, I had interpreted this (as I think most people do) as asserting that if one is in need, the person who turns up to help is your true friend. In riper years, I began to adopt the subtler interpretation that the person you choose to turn to when *you* are in crisis—the person whom you can most count on—is your true friend. While we may ask any old acquaintance for a fiver or a lift to the airport, when pain and anguish wring the brow, it is only the truest and bluest of friends—our "best friend"—to whom we turn.

The Wooster/Jeeves saga is densely populated with Bertie's friends, or, to use his most common expression, "pals." In fact, the entire saga is very "pal-centric" with nearly every story involving helping out some friend or other. Why, the very "Code of the Woosters" is about helping a friend in need.

Musing on this centrality of friendship in the Bertie Wooster stories, I began to wonder who, of all these pals, one would consider Bertie's best friend? The first step in such an investigation would be to put together a comprehensive list of the Friends of Bertie. Like all right-thinking Wodehouse scholars when embarking on a project of this kind, I began with the Ring/Jaggard *Millennium Wodehouse Concordance*—in this case, volume 6—but I found no specific list of FOBs, so I decided to assemble my own. Eschewing the Reggie Pepper stories, I came up with the following, in order of appearance:

Bruce "Corky" Corcoran
Rockmettler "Rocky" Todd
Francis "Bicky" Bickersteth
George Caffyn
Richard "Bingo" Little
Oliver "Sippy" Sipperly
Charles Edward "Biffy" Biffen
Freddie Bullivant
Hildebrand "Tuppy" Glossop
Marmaduke "Chuffy" Chuffnell
Augustus "Gussie" Fink-Nottle
Rev. Harold "Stinker" Pinker
G. D'Arcy "Stilton" Cheesewright
George Webster "Boko" Fittleworth
Claude Cattermole "Catsmeat" Potter-Pirbright
Reginald "Kipper" Herring
Harold "Ginger" Winship
Tipton Plimsoll
Orlo J. Porter

In searching for Bertie's best friend, let's begin by removing the obvious losers.

Although he and Tuppy Glossop eventually get over the little imbroglio with the rings over the swimming bath, and although they ultimately become (we assume) related by bonds of marriage, Bertie never really has a kind word for Tuppy, and he never refers to him as a "pal." Cross Tuppy off the list.

Bertie and Stilton Cheesewright certainly are not close, although when we first see them together in *Joy in the Morning*, Bertie gives the impression that they were, while at school, somewhat friendly, though he says of Stilton that he is "not one of my bosom pals." Shortly after, they are not friendly in the least, and, in the opening of *Jeeves and the Feudal Spirit*, Bertie says, "Considering that he and I have known each other since…we were so high…we ought, I suppose, to be like Damon and what's his name, but we aren't by any means." So much for Stilton.

Much of Bertie's time is involved in helping Gussie Fink-Nottle, but it is not so much for Gussie's sake as it is to keep himself out of the mulligatawny. Nonetheless, he gets mixed up with Madeleine Basset initially to help Gussie, so there must have been some sense of friendship there. But Gussie is introduced to us with the phrase, "it wasn't as if he and I were in any way bosom," and subsequent events over the course of four novels don't make them any bosomer. Scratch Gussie.

When first spotting O. J. (Orlo) Porter in a protest march, Bertie describes him thus:

> an old acquaintance…who had been on the same staircase with me at Oxford. Except for borrowing an occasional cup of sugar from one another and hulloing when we met on the stairs, we had never been close…

The events in the first half of *Aunts Aren't Gentlemen* certainly seem to bear that out. Bertie even compares him, unfavorably, to Roderick Spode. Later, however, their relations grow warmer, and at the end of the book, Bertie goes out of his way to help Orlo get his inheritance. But considering that they only just begin to call each other by their Christian names at the very end of the book, I don't think we can include him in the list of likely candidates in our search. Forget Orlo.

Having eliminated the obvious, we turn now to those with whom Bertie is actually pretty chummy, and, in doing so, one might as well begin with the first novel, *Thank You, Jeeves*, and Marmaduke, the 5th Baron Chuffnell. Certainly, Bertie has warmer feelings toward Chuffy than the four unpleasant fellows mentioned above, but he is not particularly effusive in his account of their relationship, merely remarking, "He's a fellow I've known more or less all my life, he and self having been at private school, Eton and Oxford together." Hardly a description of a deep, abiding friendship, especially when we compare it to the level of pally-ness Bertie provides for such short acquaintances as Rocky Todd ("I was fond of old Rocky"), Biffy Biffen ("we'd been lads together about town"), Freddie Bullivant ("a pal of mine"), George Caffyn (whom "I got pally with"), and especially Bicky Bickersteth, with whom he says he was "extremely pally."

The only remaining friend from the early stories (except Bingo Little, with whom we will deal shortly) is Oliver Sipperly. Bertie calls

Sippy "a dear, old friend" on more than one occasion, but, while their relationship seems as friendly as any of the others, there is nothing there to set him apart from the more casual acquaintances that Bertie seems to have inexplicably bound to himself with hoops of steel.

We can dismiss Tipton Plimsoll similarly. Bertie calls him "my American pal" (as if he didn't have any others) and has no compunction in ringing him up the morning after a celebratory night, but their friendship is really undefined. They share no stories together, and he is only used in *Aunts Aren't Gentlemen* as a plot device to get Bertie to the doctor, E. Jimpson Murgatroyd. I suspect that Wodehouse simply enjoyed, in this final novel, the idea of gratuitously creating one more of the very few, slim tendrils connecting Bertie and Jeeves to Blandings.

Catsmeat Pirbright is rather a puzzle when considered as an FOB. Bertie and he certainly seem pretty close; in *The Mating Season*, Bertie refers to their being "at private school, public school and Oxford" together, and in *Much Obliged, Jeeves*, he couples him with Kipper Herring as one of his oldest friends. But the only stories and reminiscences about Catsmeat (and there are many of them) all come from antics at the Drones—none from school. Further complicating matters is that Bertie was on quite intimate terms with Catsmeat's sister, Corky, when they were young children ("we were in the same dancing class") and throughout *The Mating Season*, he seems closer to her than he does to Catsmeat. This would indicate that Bertie and Corky are the same age, so, unless Catsmeat and Corky were twins, Bertie and Catsmeat must be separated by a number of years. It is true that in *Jeeves and the Feudal Spirit* he refers to Catsmeat as a "boyhood friend," but he is simply making excuses to Stilton for being out late, so one can dismiss that as an exaggeration invented in the moment as a hasty defense.

One must, therefore, conclude that Catsmeat is actually somewhat younger than Bertie—old enough to have been at the same school at the same time, but probably not to share each other's social sphere. This temporal anomaly is further supported by the fact that Catsmeat is playing "juvenile roles" on the stage, while Bertie is getting past that age, and that once, in *Thank You, Jeeves*, Bertie refers to him as "young Catsmeat." So the old school tie is rather loose in conjoining these two, and throughout *The Mating Season*, the only book in which they are together, there is not one word from Bertie that Catsmeat is a "friend" or "pal" or particularly close in any way.

The fact is, we can't really rely on Bertie's own words as testimony in the matter of friendship. Actions speak louder than. Although the case of Catsmeat clearly shows this, the best example of Bertie as an unreliable narrator is Bingo Little. When we are introduced to Bingo in "Jeeves in the Springtime" (later titled "Jeeves Exerts the Cerebellum"), Bertie calls him "a chap I went to school with, and we see a lot of each other still." He continues in this vein throughout the early short stories and, in "Bingo and the Little Woman," even pinpoints the beginning of their friendship when he says, "we've been pals for fifteen years."

Suddenly, however, in "Jeeves and the Impending Doom," we have a whole new history:

> [We were] pals practically from birth. Born in the same village within a couple days of one another, we went through kindergarten, Eton and Oxford together; and, grown to riper years we have enjoyed the old metrop. Full many a first-class binge in one another's company....

This doesn't quite measure up with the "pals for fifteen years" gag, and he never later refers to Bingo as his oldest friend (again, in *Much Obliged, Jeeves,* he invokes Catsmeat and Kipper to share that honor).

Most take this later recitation of the facts as read—the real and true history of Bertie and Bingo (cf. Ring and Jaggard)—so that, coupled with the number of exploits they have together, we seem to have here a pretty clear portrait of true best friends. But I think not.

Now, one could make an argument against such a contention by pointing out that we only see them together a couple of times post Bingo and Rosie's wedding, with all further Bingo exploits described by Drones other than Bertie, but I would regard this reasoning as specious on two counts. First, just because Bertie does not add any more stories to his reminiscences does not mean he does not see Bingo. We have, for instance, Bertie's comment in *Stiff Upper Lip, Jeeves* that he puts in "an occasional weekend" with Chuffy and wife Pauline, *née*

Stoker, which are all unrecorded, so any lack of further stories re Bingo is not necessarily a sign that their friendship is over.

Second, as the various narrators of the Drones Club stories are all unnamed Crumpets, Beans, and Piefaces, who is to say that one or more of them are not Bertie himself? They all write or speak very much in Bertie's style, after all. Perhaps these stories are recorded in this manner only because Bertie chose not to write them down as he was not a participant in the plot, so he merely spoke them in the club, leaving the recording of them to some other unseen hand.

I reject Bingo as a best friend for other reasons. Bingo is a taker, not a giver. Bingo is a friend in need in only one respect: He is always asking Bertie for help, and Bertie is always helping, usually reluctantly. This is not so much a friendship as some kind of neurotic co-dependency. Or, as Bertie puts it, "ever since I first knew him...I have felt a rummy feeling of responsibility for young Bingo." No. Old and dear as he is, Bingo is too self-centered to be a "best friend."

You may be forgiven if at this point you think I am leading up to some ingenious or poetic conclusion that Jeeves is Bertie's best friend. But this cannot be. Jeeves is, of course, nothing more nor less than Bertie's valet. It is true that their relationship is not the typical master-servant one (otherwise there would be no point to writing those eleven novels and several dozen short stories). But throughout, they never really step out of their traditional roles. Other metaphors for Jeeves's role in their peculiar relationship have been proffered: keeper (Aunt Agatha), nannie (Bertie himself), aunt (Usborne), spouse (me, elsewhere) to name but four. I suppose "friend" could be added to the list. But what we are looking for here is a true friend, not a metaphorical friend.

It is for this same reason we must also ignore Aunt Dahlia, even though Bertie himself refers to her as his "best friend" in "Jeeves and the Greasy Bird" and *Aunts Aren't Gentlemen*—in the latter adding the proviso "and sternest critic," indicating, I think, that he is being more clichéd than literal. In any case, an aunt is, however close, an aunt, not a friend.

I also choose not to include Sir Roderick Glossop in the list, although he has no other over-riding relationship, like valet or aunt.

Thinking of their relations in the early short stories, you may wonder why I even bring him up at all, but remember that things change during *Thank You, Jeeves*, and their friendship continues to bloom during *Jeeves in the Offing*. The last time they are together, in "Jeeves and the Greasy Bird," Bertie has been to stay with Roddy (the two at last settling on these matey sobriquets), though not really as a guest; Bertie is there to check on his cousin, who is one of Sir Roderick's patients. Nonetheless, in the story, Bertie repeatedly references him as a "pal" and describes their "hobnobbing like a couple of sailors on shore leave." In fact, much of the plot of the story involves Bertie going to great lengths to help Roddy out.

But when I think of listing the FOBs, I believe that a criterion for inclusion is that the friend must be roughly of the same age as Bertie—that they have shared the same life experiences, and that they move in the same social circles. In a word, all of Bertie's friends are Drones, or, if not actually members of that club, certainly they would not be out of place there. As Sir Roderick Glossop does not fit that profile, I think the Bertie and Roddy relationship is a non-starter, and, like Dahlia and Jeeves, I have left him off the list.

This leaves us with only Boko Fittleworth, Stinker Pinker, Ginger Winship, and Kipper Herring. Bertie consistently has very warm words for all four, and they for him. Indeed, Stinker actually says of Bertie, "He is one of my best friends."

Nonetheless, I think we can eliminate the Rev. H. P. Pinker as Bertie's "best friend." We must, after all, concentrate on actions, not words. Stinker is rather aloof throughout *The Code of the Woosters* and *Stiff Upper Lip, Jeeves*. We never see Stinker and Bertie engaged in any real camaraderie. He is consistently off-stage or standing idly by, while his bride, Stiffy Bing, dishes up plenty of dirty work for Bertie. Indeed, at the beginning of the later novel, he himself is the harbinger of what he clearly knows is bad news, viz. that Stiffy had a "job" for Bertie. Would a best friend do that?

Boko certainly seems to be a very good friend, offering to "kill the fatted calf" to welcome him in *Joy in the Morning* and being "delighted to put [Bertie] up" when Wee Nooke is immolated. Furthermore, with Boko, unlike Stinker, we see Bertie actually enjoying his company.

However, Boko has no difficulty in coercing Bertie, against his better judgment, into breaking into Steeple Bumpleigh and complains bitterly when the operation fails.

Also, much as he describes them both as buddies and pals, Bertie has some harsh words for both Boko and Stinker, including "silly ass" and "loony to the eyebrows" for the former and a "pumpkin-headed foozler" and "as pronounced a goop as ever preached about Hivites and Hittites" for the latter. Not the kind of words that indicate a rift in the lute of friendship exactly, but hardly the sort the thing one says about a best friend.

With Ginger Winship, we are definitely getting closer. No harsh words pass Bertie's mouth or pen in re this Winship. Bertie tells Aunt Dahlia that they were "like Damon and Pythias" at university and later says, "Ginger was one of my oldest buddies, not quite so old as Kipper Herring or Catsmeat Potter-Pirbright, with whom I plucked the gowans fine at prep school and university, but definitely ancient. Our rooms at Oxford were adjacent." Throughout *Much Obliged, Jeeves*, they are friendly without cessation and each helps each, as Bertie canvasses for Ginger (who is running for election at Market Snodsbury) and works on his behalf to help him disentangle himself from Florence Craye; and Ginger loans Bertie his car on a moment's notice.

But there are clues that this is not closest friendship in the world. Ginger is a bit snippy with Bertie on a couple of occasions. And their conversation, while generally amiable, is not exactly like two old buddies. Most significantly, until Ginger comes to Brinkley and Aunt Dahlia mentions this to Bertie, she did not know he and Bertie even knew each other, despite the fact that Ginger's mother was one of Dahlia's closest friends.

Contrast that with Kipper Herring. Bertie specifically mentions, at the opening of *Jeeves in the Offing*, that Kipper had been to Brinkley one summer, and, when mentioning his name to Dahlia on the phone, she has no difficulty remembering who he is.

"A life-long buddy of mine, this Herring, linked to me by what are called imperishable memories" is how Bertie introduces him to us in the very first paragraph of the novel. And those "imperishable memories"—viz. suffering through life at Malvern House run by

Aubrey Upjohn—form a substantial part of the plot of *Jeeves in the Off-ing*. The novel opens with Kipper and Bertie having breakfast together as Kipper is staying with Bertie while waiting to get into his new flat. In addition to this extended visit and Dahlia's pleasant remembrance of Kipper, there are a number of other incidents of friendship in this book that are unique in the saga.

When Bertie is coerced by Dahlia into breaking up the Willie Cream/Phyllis Mills romance, he enlists Kipper to take his place, and Kipper does so in a trice and without a murmur. Compare that to Gussie's whining about having to replace Bertie at the prize-giving.

Upon reading in the newspaper that Bertie is engaged to Bobbie Wickham, a girl to whom he has just become affianced himself, Kipper drives to Brinkley, not to excoriate Bertie, but rather to assure Bertie that "we mustn't let this thing break up our old friendship." Compare that to the behavior of Tuppy, Orlo, and Chuffy who, under similar, but far more ambiguous circumstances, attempted or threatened to ascertain the color of his insides.

Later, after Kipper and Bobbie are reconciled and when one of her hare-brained schemes falls apart, Bobbie lays into Bertie for be-ing the cause of its failure. Kipper, with no pressing reason to do so, defends Bertie to Bobbie. He actually takes his friend's side against his fiancée. That's pretty strong, especially when that fiancée is so liberally endowed with red hair and all that goes with it.

Even more incredibly, when Bertie is called upon to push Upjohn into the lake so Kipper can save him, or to say nasty things to Upjohn so Kipper can defend him, Bertie jumps to both without a hint of *nolle prosequi*. On previous occasions—with Bingo and Boko, respectively—Bertie had to be blackmailed into participation. Here, in one novel, we have repeatedly unprecedented behavior, and several examples of both interpretations of "a friend in need."

While all of this empirical evidence makes the case convincingly, I think the strongest feeling one gets for the uniqueness of this friend-ship is more ineffable: the cozy conversation between the two in the second chapter of *Jeeves in the Offing*. Too long to quote here, I encour-age you all to go back and read it. I know I am getting a little subjec-tive here, but I think no other *tête-à-tête* in the saga between Bertie and another pal—not even with Ginger Winship—has the close, almost fraternal, feel of this conversation. It has, for me, the same flavor as some of the letters to Bill Townend in *Performing Flea*, or, letting your imagination wander a little as you read it, you can almost hear Plum and Guy Bolton as they saunter together some summer afternoon down Basket Neck Lane.

Bertie Wooster is a man blessed—or cursed—with a multitude of "pals," but one can have only one "best friend." I believe that, even though he appears in only one book, Reginald "Kipper" Herring fits that bill; he is, indeed, Bertie Wooster's Best Friend Forever.

From the desk of C.
Los Angeles, CA
20 November, 2017

Thanks for the Books

Here, then, is the Ur text. The first, in this case, shall be last. Adapted, edited, and abbreviated, but with all essential points intact, this is where all of Elliott's and my attempts at Wodehousean exegesis began: as an undergraduate thesis, written by him at the University of Toronto in 1975-76. In its original state, it was a massive work and one of which he was deservedly proud. It put forth a theory concerning Wodehouse's development as a writer that became the prism through which he would view Wodehouse's writings ever after and which was referenced in nearly every talk given and article written by him since.

The basic thesis of the paper—that Wodehouse's writing could be definitively divided into three periods, with the Early period ending in 1923 with the publication of *Leave it to Psmith* and the Middle period ending with *Full Moon* in 1947—still holds. As an undergraduate thesis composed by a twenty-two-year-old some twenty-five years before the earliest essay included in this book, it clearly lacked the style and polish his later work would attain. Also, it had been written during a kind of Wodehousean Dark Age, at a time when there was comparatively little critical source material or secondary scholarship available. Unable to locate a copy of, for example, Richard Usborne's seminal *Wodehouse at Work*, Elliott was restricted to only six then-extant reference works. As a result, the final piece contained a number of errors and omissions.

Nevertheless, it was, particularly at the time, a heroic piece of scholarship and a labor of love, and for many years afterward, Elliott had nursed a dream of publishing it as a stand-alone piece of Wodehouse exegesis. That had never happened, but as plans for this book developed, the subject was raised again: What price "The Growth of Sweetness and Light?" As it was the first Wodehouse piece written by either of us, surely it should be included. But where and in what form? When we were considering a chronological collection, it would of course be the first chapter of the book. But that may have been asking a bit much of a general reader. We considered including it as an appendix as well, but eventually concluded it was just too long, or too long at least to be considered appropriate for inclusion in its original form. In the end, Elliott edited it down by nearly a third, removed nearly all footnotes, references, and other academic impedimenta and, in general, made it more accessible without losing the gist.

I remember the day that I opened a special delivery envelope and laid eyes on the fabled thesis for the first time. I had just moved to New York, an itinerant actor who had never so much as seen a thesis before. Opening it, I saw the inscription: "For Curt Armstrong—without whose conversation and cognac this essay would never have been thought of. Thanks for the books. —Elliott."

Clearly Elliott was as moved by his accomplishment as I was: there is no other explanation for him ending a sentence with a preposition. That original copy has remained one of the cornerstones of my collection ever since. And now, with a little editorial legerdemain, "The Growth of Sweetness and Light: A Study of the Novels of P. G. Wodehouse," finally enters the Canon.

THE GROWTH
OF SWEETNESS AND LIGHT:
A STUDY OF THE NOVELS
OF P. G. WODEHOUSE

Elliott Milstein

This is an abridged version of a thesis written at St Michael's College in the University of Toronto, 1975-76.

I. INTRODUCTION: THE THREE PERIODS

In this paper, my task will be to divide the books of P. G. Wodehouse into three distinct Periods: Early, Middle and Late. I will examine and delineate the three periods, dealing with various aspects of the books. I will approach Wodehouse's development almost exclusively through his novels, especially his "sagas." I will look, in particular, at the two chief sagas, the Blandings Castle saga and, especially, the Wooster/Jeeves saga (the latter has a very important role in Wodehouse's development).

The Early Period (1902-1923) was a period of experimentation for Wodehouse. He tried many different types of style, character, and attitude. It is only in this period that any distinct difference can be seen between romance and farce in the novels. Some critics have tried to find this split in the entire Canon, but, beginning with *Leave it to Psmith* in 1923, this distinction can no longer be maintained. It is an exciting period to study because of the spirit of experimentation, but it is relatively unimportant to this discussion as it has little effect on the Middle and Late Periods. I will, therefore, deal with it briefly at the outset, noting only three books that have an important bearing on the rest of this discussion.

It is in delineating the Middle and Late Periods that I propose to spend most of my time. Other scholars have noticed the sudden change in Wodehouse's writing with *Leave it to Psmith*, but none notice that in *Full Moon* (1947), there is another equally distinct, if more subtle break, beginning his Late Period. We know that the first third of *Full Moon* was written while Wodehouse was interned in a Nazi internment camp, and the book was finished on his release. As we shall see, it is between Chapters Four and Five of *Full Moon*, the time of his release, that the Late Period began.

For some years, beginning with *Full Moon*, Wodehouse received much criticism from the reviewers. (I will assume that this criticism was based entirely on his writing, not on his radio broadcasts during the War.) The critics cried either, "Wodehouse is losing his grip," or "Wodehouse has become a bore." The only change they could see was a negative one.

His defenders, and there were a few, were quick to argue that nothing had changed; Wodehouse could still crack them through the covers. A. P. Ryan wrote,

> The only sign to be found in the books since the War that time has marched on is that, here and there, a date has changed, a gag been brought up to date.... Based thus on a static scenario, Mr. Wodehouse has made his comic spirit timeless and carried it to perfection.

In arguing thus, Mr. Ryan, who certainly meant well, did P. G. Wodehouse a great disservice. Much had changed in Wodehouse's writing since the War; the scenario was not static, and rather than point out the shift, he, and others, kept readers from seeing what Wodehouse was doing. (It is, of course, likely that nobody noticed.) It wasn't until the late 1950s that Wodehouse was once again called "Master" and began to receive uniformly good reviews again, but only because people were beginning to enjoy his books once more, not because they had noticed the new style and approach.

We shall see that this new approach can be simply (!) characterized by three things: 1) a reduction of emphasis on romance; 2) a greater emphasis on comedy, often in a wilder form; and 3) a greater reliance on a Bertie Wooster approach. This final Period ends with his last novel, *Aunts Aren't Gentlemen* (1974), which I see as a possible beginning of a fourth period, one that Wodehouse never lived to bring to fruition.

II. THE EARLY PERIOD

The first years of Wodehouse's literary career were dedicated to books, short stories and newspaper sketches in various styles and under various pseudonyms. In short, he wrote whatever he thought he could sell. Because of these financial considerations, not much importance should be placed on his writing at this time. Nonetheless, we can take a brief look at this beginning to note how Wodehouse was developing his craft before proceeding to the central argument, which is the delineation of the Middle and Late Periods.

Love Among the Chickens (1906) is generally cited as Wodehouse's first mature book, but, though it is his first book for adults, it is not a particularly good effort. Wodehouse himself realized this and revised it for its reprinting in 1921. Most scholars emphasize the importance of *Love Among the Chickens*, for in it Ukridge, the first Wodehouse character, appears. But this creation should not be over-estimated as Ukridge has no successor. Jeremy Garnet, the book's narrator, on the other hand, is the first of all the main male romantic leads—all later romantic leads are derived from him up to 1923. For the birth of the true Wodehouse character, we must look to Rupert Ronald Eustace Psmith, the precursor of all of Wodehouse's principal male characters, from Ronnie Fish to Uncle Fred, from Bingo Little to Jeeves.

Psmith makes his first appearance in *Mike* (1909), a boys' school story, but right from the beginning we can tell—although Wodehouse was not to find out for some years—that destiny was to mark Psmith for more important feats than playing cricket and ragging. He is unlike any other schoolboys in Wodehouse's fiction, from Tony Graham of *The Pothunters* (1902) to Mike Jackson himself. Even at Sedleigh, we notice a grown-up air about Psmith, as in his private conversation with the head-master at the end of the book:

"Strictly between ourselves, sir—"

Privately, the headmaster found Psmith's man-to-man attitude somewhat disconcerting, but he said nothing.

"I should not like it to go any further, sir."

"Well, Smith?"

"I don't want anybody to know, sir. This is strictly between ourselves."

"I think you are sometimes apt to forget, Smith, the proper relations existing *between* boy and—Well, never mind that for the present."

...

"Not a bad sort" said Psmith meditatively to himself, as he walked downstairs. "By no means a bad sort. I must drop in from time to time and cultivate him."

It is significant that he is the only character we see both in school and in the real world after his superannuation. He is the only character who is both a member of the Drones Club and of the Senior Conservative Club. But Psmith's real importance comes later, when he visits Blandings Castle.

The next important book for Wodehouse was *A Gentleman of Leisure* (1910), a book greatly under-rated by most Wodehouse scholars. Here is the first true romantic comedy in the Wodehouse Canon. Where *Love Among the Chickens* failed, *A Gentleman of Leisure* succeeds. The comic elements are well integrated with the serious aspects, and the point of view is consistent, as opposed to *Love Among the Chickens*, which begins in third person, shifts suddenly to the first person, and ends with a short play. David Jasen, in his biography of Wodehouse, says of *A Gentleman of Leisure*,

This was the first humorous story to be set in a stately home in Shropshire, and it featured an amiable but dim peer, the first in a long line of Drones, a tycoon, a formidable aunt, a pretty but foolish girl and a butler—the standard main ingredients for future Wodehouse novels.

It also introduces the underworld motif, which Wodehouse would use for the rest of his career. As in *The Prince and Betty* (1912), *Psmith Journalist* (the 1915 reworking of *The Prince and Betty*), and *The Little Nugget* (1913)—all of which follow—in *A Gentleman of Leisure*, corruption is treated seriously and crime humorously. Later, the corruption motif will disappear, but crime, especially "the confidence game," will continue to be treated in an increasingly light vein, as in *Money for Nothing* (1928), *Uncle Fred in the Springtime* (1939), and *Pearls, Girls and Monty Bodkin* (1973).

The last book I will examine in this period is the first of the Blandings Castle stories: *Something Fresh* (1915). It introduces Lord Emsworth; Beach, that supreme butler; Rupert Baxter; and Freddie Threepwood. Although these characters were to undergo certain changes before the second book of the saga would be written, their basic personalities are outlined here.

Something Fresh was the first Wodehouse book, indeed one of the few books by a British author up to this time, to offer detailed accounts of every aspect of British society, from earls and dukes, to the middle class, to the servants, to the London low-life, and even the visiting American millionaires. We see both sides of the green baize door, both sides of the Atlantic, and the fashionable and shadier sides of London. This panoramic view distracts, at times, from the important aspects of the story, but it was a bold attempt for Wodehouse, and, on the whole, it succeeds.

Freddie Threepwood, too, is the first true member of the Drones Club. Reggie Pepper, created in 1911, is later converted into Bertie Wooster, the most famous Drone, but he does not come officially on the scene until 1915.

Wodehouse's first-person narratives do not strictly follow the pattern of development I am showing in this paper, but the Wooster/Jeeves stories have an important effect, especially in the Late Period. The other narrators of first-person stories were all created before 1926 and never developed as characters. They are all monomaniacs: the Oldest Member is thoroughly potty about golf, Mr. Mulliner about his family, and James Corcoran about Ukridge, so they have a very limited point of view.

Bertie Wooster is not similarly handicapped. Although he is not a very bright young man, he does have a variety of interests: women, food, school, horse-racing, his friends, his family (specifically his aunts), travel, and so on. Also, with the exception of *Laughing Gas* (1936), a very bizarre and atypical Wodehouse book, the Wooster/Jeeves saga is the only first-person narrative in novel form. This gives Wodehouse room to expand and develop, and this development parallels closely the other Wodehouse books, with some interesting differences, which I will examine later.

Bertie Wooster's somewhat flippant attitude toward love becomes manifest by 1921, although it is not until 1923 that this will be true of the third-person narratives. It is one of the characteristics of the Middle Period.

Another characteristic is the introduction of a new speech pattern and greater interest in the jargon of the young men about town. Bertie, however, will continue his traditional British middle-class *entre deux guerres* slang until *Very Good, Jeeves* (1930), when he starts using expressions like "eggs and b." and "teuf-teuf." Bertie is also addicted to popular ideas of his day, such as Couéism (which Wodehouse parodies a good deal in most of his books) and the notion that fish is good for the brain. He stops falling in love after 1930, but is constantly getting engaged. His attitude toward women is always chivalrous, but distinctly unromantic.

Indeed, there are many attitudes expressed in the Wooster/Jeeves saga that do not occur in the other books. Throughout the Middle Period especially, there are many aspects of this major saga that do not occur in the third-person narratives, as Wodehouse develops it along its own path. However, in the Late Period, these aspects begin to appear in the other books, as we shall see.

It is clear, then, that the works of the Early Period share common characteristics, but that these characteristics change over time. Through a review and analysis of these characteristics as seen in Wodehouse's use of character, structure, patterns, and language, the remainder of this work will seek to clearly categorize the novels following *Leave it to Psmith* into his Middle Period, which begins in 1923 with that novel, and his Late Period, which begins during his writing of *Full Moon* in 1945.

III. CHARACTER

Most scholars notice an important change in Wodehouse's writing around the time of *Leave it to Psmith* (1923), but none mention that an equally important change takes place during the writing of *Full Moon* (1947). In this section, we will examine the changes concerning the characters in these two works and the works that follow them. In *Leave it to Psmith*, the change is readily attributable to Psmith; in *Full Moon*, it is somewhat more difficult to find, and only by studying Psmith's effect on the Middle Period can we see what Wodehouse is doing in the Late Period.

We last left Psmith smoldering away at Sedleigh in our discussion of the Early Period. There are two Psmith novels after *Mike* (1909) that show our hero in a more grown-up World: *Psmith in the City* (1910), where he is working in a London bank, and *Psmith Journalist* (1915), where he has effectively taken over a small New York newspaper. Psmith, in all three books, is the same languid, talky character. He is unique in the Wodehouse Canon and does not really affect Wodehouse's writing until he arrives at Blandings.

Wodehouse critic Richard J. Voorhees points out that Psmith's distinct language, which "pushes the poetry around, mixes slang with classy diction, and indulges in conscious malapropisms,"[1] becomes a source of the four major styles of speech in Wodehouse: 1) the clever young hero or "such perennial undergraduates as Uncle Fred or Lancelot [*sic*] Threepwood"; 2) Wodehouse's morons, such as Freddie Threepwood, Bingo Little, and Bertie Wooster; 3) Jeeves, whose style of speech, regardless of subject matter, "stems from the formal strain in Psmith's"; and 4) "Wodehouse's own" narrative voice.[2]

But Voorhees then goes on to say, "The voice of Psmith is first heard in the last of the school novels and next in *Psmith in the City*. From then on, with negligible exceptions, Wodehouse will never write in the lucid but straightforward narrative style of the school stories."

This, I think, misplaces Psmith's most important characteristic, which is not so much the exuberance of his verbosity as it is his mild, almost condescending approach to life. Wodehouse's manner in *The*

---

1   Richard Voorhees, *P.G. Wodehouse* (New York: Twayne, 1966), 84.
2   Ibid, 84-5.

Little Nugget (1913), *Something Fresh* (1915), *The Coming of Bill* (1919), or *The Adventures of Sally* (1922), to name but a few, could hardly be called Psmithian. It is not until *Leave it to Psmith*, when he mixes two sagas together for the first time, that Wodehouse's attitude begins to resemble Psmith's. This is the dawning of a new era in Wodehouse; it is the beginning of the Middle Period.

Now although Bertie Wooster can be seen as an extension of Psmith throughout the Middle Period, by 1946, he has developed into a character that bears very little resemblance to the Old Etonian. While Psmith is mildly detached from the events that go on around him, Bertie is frantically trying to extricate himself from the "bouillon" or "mulligatawny." It is this frenzy that becomes key-note for the Late Period characters.

For example, Galahad Threepwood, who, in *Summer Lightning* (1929) and *Heavy Weather* (1933), never loses his poise and control and always views the problems concerning his brother's pig, the Empress of Blandings, in an amused and even condescending fashion, is, in *Full Moon* and *Pigs Have Wings* (1952), constantly losing his temper and has a very strong vested interest in the future of that pre-eminent sow. In *Heavy Weather*, he becomes angry with Ronnie Fish for breaking his engagement with Sue Brown, a matter of love; but in *Full Moon*, he reaches new levels of violent rhetoric when Freddie Threepwood ruins his own plans.

Love—I will discuss this in greater detail later—is treated in a much lighter tone after *Leave it to Psmith*. From 1923 on, no distinction can be discerned between the comic and the romantic elements in Wodehouse's stories. This attitude stems mostly from the romantic hero himself. Previously, he had little or nothing to do with the humorous scenes, and there was certainly nothing funny about his actual wooing of the woman he loved. Quite the opposite is true of Psmith. He is the center of all of the humorous scenes in *Leave it to Psmith* (with the exception of the famous flower-pot sequence, in which he takes a minor part in Baxter's bumblings), and his proposal to Eve is one of the funniest scenes in the novel.

Although this tendency toward humorous wooing does not hold true for Wodehouse's next romantic hero Bill West, beginning with

Sam Shotter, it becomes more and more greatly pronounced (cf Mike Cardinal in *Spring Fever* [1948], etc.). If the romantic hero is serious, there is a *deus ex machina* in the form of Galahad or Uncle Fred, who retains the light tone, and though the young lover may take himself seriously, the reader does not. Wodehouse manipulates our feelings to persuade us to take a humorous view.

After *Full Moon*, the romantic hero falls into the background. His seriousness just isn't funny enough anymore. In *Full Moon*, the work that Freddie Threepwood and Galahad do on his behalf take up more room than Bill Lister himself. The romance and the comedy are no longer tied together, but the comedy is given supreme importance.

From *Leave it to Psmith* on, all female leads are in the Eve Halliday mold. She is usually short, pretty—but only beautiful to the man who falls in love with her—she has a jaunty walk, an uptilted chin, an I'm-ready-for-you-world attitude. If she is ever reduced to tears, it is only for the moment; then she is herself again.

This is not true of the Bertie Wooster books. Bertie, after 1925, is a confirmed bachelor, almost a misogynist. To Bertie, women are either big, beefy girls like Honoria Glossop; or saccharine, droopy girls like Madeline Bassett; or, if they are in the Eve Halliday line, they are too much so, like Stiffy Byng, who expects too much from a fellow.

After *Full Moon*, the heroines of the Wooster/Jeeves books remain the same, but in other books they undergo a slight change. Their physical beauty is generally played down, or even made into a joke. In *Something Fishy* (1957), although Bill Hollister is knocked base over apex by the sound of Jane Benedick's voice over the telephone, when he first sees her, he classifies her as "rather pretty." In the Middle Period, during the tender moment, the girl always appears at her best. Not so in *Something Fishy*:

> How lovely she was, he was thinking, though in forming this view he was in actual fact mistaken. A girl cannot stand over a kitchen stove on a warm June night, cooking a chicken and two veg., not to mention clear soup, and other delicacies, and remain natty. Jane's face was flushed and her hair disheveled, and across one cheek there was a smudge of what appeared to be blacklead.

In the Middle Period, the male leads, at least physically, differ more than the female leads. They may be short and pink, like Ronnie Fish, or tall and lissome, like Hugo Carmody, or large and strong (usually ex-football or -rugby players) like Bill West. They might be shy and diffident, overpowering, smooth and sophisticated, or quiet and rugged, but they are always good looking.

This changes with *Full Moon*. The large and strong hero moves from the rugby player to the boxer, who, during his pugilist career, had attained a cauliflower ear and a nose that changes directions several times on its journey from glabella to philtrum, or he might just be plain or unattractive without any further help. Bill Lister is the first of these heroes, and once again, the result is comical:.

> The face that gazed from the photograph was not that of a strictly handsome man. It was, indeed, that of one who would have had to receive a considerable number of bisques to make it worth his while to enter even the most minor of beauty contests. The nose was broad, the ears prominent, the chin prognathous. This might, in fact, have been the photograph of a kindly gorilla.

And Bill Lister is only the first of many. Stanwood Cobbold, the hero of the very next book, *Spring Fever*, looks like a hippopotamus. In short, after 1945, physical beauty is ignored or made comical.

Thus, in the Late Period, Wodehouse makes his romantic characters funnier in appearance and pushes them into the background to make room for more characters who, having little or nothing to do with the romantic elements, are, nonetheless, main characters and interesting for their comic elements.

Other wildly comical characters are created during the Late Period, such as Howard Saxby—the senile publisher in *Cocktail Time* (1958)—and Henry Paradene—the desperately impecunious squire of *Company for Henry* (1967). Wodehouse's standard lunatics, like Uncle Fred, become even wilder, and even Jeeves, whose machinations during the Middle Period might have been unorthodox but always respectable, loosens up a bit in the Late Period.

In the earlier books, Jeeves always saves the situation by working through Bertie; he is always Bertie Wooster's man. He suggests schemes based on "the psychology of the individual," or puts Bertie through hell because the young master won't give up his purple socks or white mess-jacket. But he always acts in the role of the valet. In the Late Period, Jeeves acts outside this role. Thus, in *The Mating Season* (1947), we see him cosh Constable Evans, in *Jeeves and the Feudal Spirit* (1954), he imitates Bertie on the telephone to save him the embarrassment of handling the phone call, and in *Stiff Upper Lip, Jeeves* (1963), he assumes the personality of Inspector Witherspoon of Scotland Yard in order to save Bertie. This kind of behavior is expected more from Uncle Fred, a confirmed loony (ask his nephew Pongo), who actually does the same thing for his friend "Beefy" Bastable (under the name Inspector Jervis) in *Cocktail Time*. But for Jeeves, this behavior is unheard of. It is all part of the greater emphasis on comedy in the Late Period.

Beginning with *Leave it to Psmith*, Wodehouse began to make every character count and weed out unnecessary characters. This is quite a conscious effort on his part throughout the Middle Period, as we can see by the letter he wrote his friend William Townend on November 4, 1923:

> The principle I always go on in writing a long story is to think of the characters in terms of actors in a play. I say to myself, when I invent a good character for an early scene: "If this were a musical comedy we should have to get somebody like Leslie Henson to play this part, and if he found out that all he had was a short scene in act one, he would walk out. How, therefore, can I twist the story so as to give him more to do and keep him alive till the fall of the curtain?" This generally works well and improves the story.

Critics tend to dwell a great deal on the influence of Wodehouse's career in the theatre on his other prose writing, and this passage alone gives them justification. It is not my intention, however, to note the whys and wherefores, but only the whats and hows of Wodehouse's writing.

Wodehouse changes his attitude completely after 1945. He often introduces a character for one short scene or just a few comical lines. If we may call the technique he outlines above "theatrical," we may call his new technique in the Late Period "cinematic," though there is no evidence that his involvement in films in the thirties is the cause of this change; however, the use of these small parts certainly has a cinematic quality to it.

The first instance of this in the Canon is the case of Beach the butler in *Full Moon*. In previous Blandings Castle stories, Beach is an integral part of every plot; his character, his actions, his feelings are explored in depth. He is as much a part of the castle as its battlements and turrets, and we are normally introduced to him immediately, follow him throughout the book, and hear his stately and reserved comments at the end.

For most of *Full Moon*, however, he is conspicuously absent. He suddenly turns up over halfway through the book—at the end of chapter seven—for six short lines. The effect is humorous, but highly unexpected in light of Wodehouse's previous attitude to small, "meaty" parts. His attitude has changed; this is the Late Period.

Wodehouse continues to bring in characters like this throughout the Late Period, usually characters we have already met in earlier books. Hence, we see Mr. Donaldson briefly in *Pigs Have Wings*, Percy Pilbeam briefly in *Something Fishy*, Madeline Basset briefly in *The Mating Season*, and many more.

In *Leave it to Psmith*, as the important characters are given more to do, the cast of unimportant characters is made more abstract. Each guest and servant is named in *Something Fresh*, while in *Leave it to Psmith*, though we know they are there, we are never properly introduced to them. Wodehouse does not want to distract us from his main characters. Let us compare a passage from each book. Consider first an Early Period scene from *Something Fresh*, in which Mrs. Twemlow, the housekeeper, is introducing Ashe Marson to the other servants:

> "Mr. Judson, Mr. Marson. Mr. Judson is the Honourable Frederick's gentleman."
>
> "You have not the pleasure of our Freddie's acquaintance as yet, I take it, Mr. Marson?" observed Mr. Judson genially, a smooth-

faced, lazy-looking young man. "Freddie repays inspection."

"Mr. Marson, permit me to introduce you to Mr. Ferris, Lord Stockheath's gentleman."

Mr. Ferris, a dark, cynical man with a high forehead, shook Ashe by the hand.

"Happy to meet you, Mr. Marson."

"Miss Willoughby, this is Mr. Marson, who will take you into dinner. Miss Willoughby is Lady Mildred Mant's lady. As of course you are aware, Lady Mildred, our eldest daughter, married Colonel Horace Mant."

. . .

He had just been introduced to an appallingly statuesque lady of the name of Chester, Lady Ann Warblington's own maid, and his somewhat hazy recollections of Joan's lectures on Below Stairs precedence left him with the impression that this was his destined partner.

Note the contrast with a similarly-peopled Middle Period scene from *Leave it to Psmith*, in which Wodehouse describes the preparation for the County Ball at Shifley:

Blandings Castle was astir from roof to hall. Lights blazed, voices shouted, bells rang. All over the huge building there prevailed a vast activity like that of a barracks on the eve of the regiment's departure for abroad.... In the bedrooms on every floor, Reggies, doubtful at the last moment about their white ties, were feverishly arranging new ones; Berties brushed their already glistening hair; and Claudes shouted to Archies along the passages insulting inquiries as to whether they had been sneaking their handkerchiefs. Valets skimmed like swallows up and down corridors, maids fluttered in and out of rooms in aid of Beauty in distress.

In a much shorter passage without mentioning any particulars, Wodehouse is able, in *Leave it to Psmith*, to impart the numbers of people, their types, the size of the Castle and the chaos going on. He is able to suggest without stating, and thus does not cloud the reader's mind with unimportant detail.

After *Full Moon*, Wodehouse goes on to phase out important characters as well. Even if they have important parts in the story, if they are not comical, we generally do not meet them. So although Bunny Farringdon is engaged to Johnny Pearce in *Cocktail Time*, and all of Uncle Fred's work is ultimately on their behalf, we never see Bunny. From what we hear of her, she sounds like a typical Wodehouse heroine whom we have seen time and time again and do not need to see again if she has nothing special to do.

Similarly, Veronica Wedge, whom we meet in *Full Moon*, is not necessary in the sequel, *Galahad at Blandings* (1965). The only comic effect she offers is her supreme stupidity, which was thoroughly exploited in *Full Moon*; there is no more comedy to be extracted from it.

The unusual aspect of all this is that Wodehouse has created such a strong atmosphere of these characters' presence that the reader feels that he has actually met them. Wodehouse used this effect in some early short stories, notably "Jeeves and the Yule-tide Spirit" (1927), where Tuppy Glossop and Bobbie Wickham are ever-present, but never seen. With a first-person narrator like Bertie, the effect is easily achieved since he is hobnobbing with these characters, but only reporting the results of the meetings. In the third-person books, it is much more difficult to accomplish, but Wodehouse does it with such ability and success that the reader hardly notices that the book is one or two characters short.

Thus we can see that in the Middle Period, the love interest becomes more comical. Wodehouse's attitude toward life in general beginning with *Leave it to Psmith* is light and frothy. There are no more earth-shaking problems, like broken marriages, graft, or alcoholism. Imposture, once used by Wodehouse characters for the purposes of theft or kidnapping (e.g. Lord Wisbeach in *Piccadilly Jim* [1917]), is now used to further wooing, and will be used continually for that purpose only. *Leave it to Psmith* is the crossroads for the new use of this dramatic device: Psmith is successful in his deception while trying to win Eve Halliday, but Edward Cootes fails when he arrives at the castle (under the assumed character Wodehouse had earlier used for Psmith) intending to steal Lady Constance's necklace. No character, after 1923, tries to sneak in anywhere, posing as someone else, merely for material gain.

In the Late Period, the romantic and comic elements seem to split again. The romantic heroes are just as earnest, beginning with *Full Moon*, as the Early Period romantic heroes had been, only now they are de-emphasized or used as "straight-men" by the comic characters. And the comic characters themselves become even more comical.

This subtle move away from romance with greater and greater emphasis on humor can be seen best through a study and comparison of the structure of the books of the Middle and Late Periods.

IV. STRUCTURE

Leave it to Psmith (1923) was Wodehouse's first book with a tightly structured storyline. It is true that in its first printing in *The Saturday Evening Post*, the ending was not quite right, but after "a stream of letters cursing it,"[3] he revised it, and *Leave it to Psmith* remains one of Wodehouse's best books in terms of structure.

Middle Period novels are so constructed that all major characters, and all premises upon which the story will turn, are introduced and outlined in the first two or three chapters. The rest of the novel deals with the characters coping with the various conflicts that arise. The spring winds tighter and tighter, the plot thickens, until it all comes right in the end, usually through some highly improbable circumstance.

This structure changes perceptibly in *Full Moon* (1947). In previous Blandings Castle stories, when an impostor comes to the castle, and at least one usually does, he stays an impostor until the end; the problems which arise from this deception make up the greater part of the comedy in the story. One person, usually Baxter, discovers the imposture, tries to expose it, but is blackmailed into silence. Baxter gets an ally or two, who in turn get allies, until everyone at the castle (except, of course, Lord Emsworth) knows the man or woman is a fraud but cannot spill the beans to anyone else. This works best in *Leave it to Psmith* and *Uncle Fred in the Springtime* (1939), where both Uncle Fred and Psmith have the style and class to carry it off.

In *Full Moon*, the impostor, Bill Lister, does not have the style or the class, and it is Gally who carries it off for him. Further, the plot does not thicken due to his imposture because when he is found out,

---

3   P. G. Wodehouse, *Performing Flea* (London: Herbert Jenkins, 1953), 20.

he is thrown out of the house by Lady Hermione. Bill, with Gally's aid, merely insinuates himself into Blandings again and again. The story is not as tight as in previous books. Also, most of the humor in the novel does not arise from Bill's impostures, but from Tipton Plimsoll's delusion that Bill is a specter of alcoholic delirium.

It is no wonder that the majority of critics did not like *Full Moon*. It does not capture the reader and tax his attention in the way that, say, *Uncle Fred in the Springtime* does. But I think we can see that Wodehouse did not do this by mistake or because he was "losing his grip." It was generally the love story that called for the complex plot, and Wodehouse was moving away from the emphasis on love. The complexity of the Late Period novels comes from thefts of the Empress, who's got the jewels, or what the Molloys will do next. Therefore, the funny scenes of the Late Period stories are funny by themselves, not because the circumstances leading up to them create the humor.

Once again, I think we can turn to the Wooster/Jeeves saga for the clue to this change. In 1946, Wodehouse wrote to Townend that "in a Jeeves story every line has to have some entertainment value," and I think he was beginning to realize that this was true of every kind of story. The days of the big buildups were over. In the Middle Period, only scenes from the Wooster/Jeeves books could be taken out of the story and remain funny, so the prize-giving scene in *Right Ho, Jeeves* (1934) and the bedroom scene in *The Code of the Woosters* (1938) were read and re-read by people almost as separate short stories.

In the Late Period, this attitude is introduced in the third person novels as well. The reader need not know anything about Sam Bagshot to enjoy the scene at the pig-sty in Chapter Eight of *Galahad at Blandings* (1965), where Sam discovers that the Empress has a hangover instead of swine fever as averred by George Cyril Wellbeloved, thus causing Lord Emsworth to panic. With Emsworth's relief comes his invitation to Sam stay at the castle and Gally's sudden and unnecessary complication of the situation by introducing Sam as an imposter. Of course, the reader must know all about Emsworth, Wellbeloved, and Galahad. And perhaps that is a clue to the change. In the Middle Period, the Wooster/Jeeves saga was the only one that depended heavily on the earlier books of the saga. By *Full Moon*, the steady

Wodehouse reader will have been to Blandings more than five times; he need not be introduced to all his favorite characters again. While Bertie Wooster can excuse himself to the "old customers" while going over old ground for the "new chappies," Wodehouse must learn to say what he had said before in a funnier way. I shall show this greater emphasis on saga more in the next section.

Another interesting development is Wodehouse's use of time. In the Early Period, a novel might cover any amount of time, from several days to several years. In the Middle Period, he generally structures the story to take place within a week, rarely more than ten days, and often as little as three.

In the Late Period, Wodehouse often breaks his own rule regarding time structure. He does not expand the story to months or years, but often has an introductory paragraph taking place sometime before the main action, as in *Something Fishy* (1957), or tags an ending taking place sometime after the main action, as in *French Leave* (1956).

Oddly enough, though fooling about with time more in the Late Period, Wodehouse still follows his amusing practice of placing all his action in the summer. It might be assumed that this is because the warm season is the most appropriate for wooing, but I think the cause lies much deeper. Wodehouse, like all his male leads, is at heart a schoolboy. Richard Voorhees points out that the Code of the Woosters "is that of a schoolboy,"[4] but really, the underlying code of all of Wodehouse's characters is the old schoolboy ethics. So although the schoolboys of Wodehouse's early stories have all their fun while still in school, the mature Wodehouse reflects that the only truly free time a boy has is during the summer holidays. Winter is a time for work, but summer is a time for adventure, and there is nothing more adventurous for a Wodehouse hero in his mid-twenties than falling in love.

In the Middle Period, there are always two pairs of lovers per book (sometimes three), one pair taking the main role, while the other stays more or less in the background. We always see the main couple together, and it is their love story in which we are most interested. The other is used as foil, comic relief, and often, when a rift occurs in both lutes simultaneously, the lovers change partners until everything is straightened

---

4   Richard Voorhees, *P. G. Wodehouse* (New York: Twayne, 1966), 113.

out. The main couple is often already engaged before the book opens, but they always have, at least, met before.

Sometimes this point is stretched. In *Bill the Conqueror* (1924), Flick Sheridan fell in love with Bill West when she was sixteen, when he saved her from drowning. In *Sam the Sudden* (1925), Sam Shotter fell in love with a picture of Ann Derrick while marooned in a hut in Canada. The most forced instance is the case of Joe Vanringham of *Summer Moonshine* (1938), who claims that he was married to Jane Abbot in another life. In the secondary romance, we see the two lovers meet for the first time and then rarely again until they announce their engagement. If there is a third romance, it is between two lower- or servant-class characters, one of whom we never see.

Something unusual happens to this structure in *Full Moon*. Bill Lister and Prudence Garland are no doubt the main love interest. They are planning a surreptitious wedding at the opening of the story, and it is their love story we are most interested in. But we never see them together in the book! Tipton Plimsoll and Veronica Wedge make up the other contingent. We see them meet for the first time, their love story is much more comical, but it is them we see together throughout the book. In later books, such as *Cocktail Time* (1958), the low-life romance actually has precedence in the plot.

It is, in fact, impossible to distinguish between main love interests and secondary love interests any more. They are all equal, and, in comparison with the earlier books, unimportant. It is unusual from *Full Moon* on to find a book in which any lovers meet more than once, if that.

Let us compare two nearly identical scenes, one from each period. In both cases, the woman is engaged to someone unsuited for her and spurns the advances of the man who loves her, and it is at this point where the heart melts. Lord Uffenham instigates the second proposal scene by recalling how well the first one worked and repeats it, but Wodehouse's treatment is very different. The first passage is from 1942's *Money in the Bank*:

> The tobacco jar was one of those large, thick, bulging tobacco jars.
>
> ...
>
> Dolly, moreover, though of apparently frail physique, was

stronger than she looked. She possessed good, muscular wrists and a nice sense of timing. The result was that one blow... was amply sufficient. Jeff's eyes rolled heavenwards, his knees buckled under him, and he sagged to the floor.

And, as he did so, Anne sprang forward with an anguished scream and flung herself on the remains.

"Jeff." she cried. "Oh, Jeff, darling!"

Considering her views, strongly held and freely expressed, regarding this young man, such agitation may appear strange...but it is a well-known fact...that at times like this the feminine outlook tends to extreme and sudden alteration.

The second passage is from 1957's *Something Fishy*:

"Lord love a duck, I can see the scene as plainly as if it had happened yesterday. There was Jeff squaring away at Molloy, and Mrs. Molloy...upped with the jar and let him have it. Like this," said Lord Uffenham, and lumbered to the door. "Jane," he called. "Jay-un."

"Yes?"

"Cummere. Young Holloway's had an accident."

. . .

It was some little time later that Bill, waking from a disordered nightmare...became aware that someone was standing at his side.

. . .

"Was that you?" he said coldly.

"Hey?"

"Did you hit me with that tobacco jar?"

"Yress, that's right. Bring the young folks together, that's what I say. As I anticipated, it worked... up she comes and, seeing your prostrate form, flings herself on it and kisses yer. The usual routine."

Well, we've seen the scene before, and we need not see it again, so Wodehouse passes over it. By the advent of the Late Period, we've seen over sixty engagements in the Wodehouse Canon, so there is no need to show any more; thus, a romantic scene that Wodehouse once would have shown in detail is now left out completely.

That is not to say that love is ignored in the Late Period; it is always there and often still forms the main core of the plot. In fact, in some respects as I will show, the climate of love is more pervasive than ever; it just isn't central. In the earlier books, as soon as the love interest is sorted out, the novel ends. This is not wholly true of the novels of the Late Period. In *Something Fishy*, for instance, the real main interest is the tontine, and though the love angle is fully resolved about three-quarters of the way through the book, there is still the tontine to be settled, so the story goes on.

V. PATTERNS

I have been at some pains up to this point to show how Wodehouse has de-emphasized the romantic aspect of his novels in the Late Period. At this point of our discussion, we run into something of a paradox in this matter. The short piece of dialogue between Mr. Bunting and Jerry Shoesmith at the end of *Frozen Assets* (1964) sums up Wodehouse's attitude in the Late Period:

"...Are you, too, going to be married?"

"I am."

"So, it appears, is everybody...It's like some kind of epidemic."

Indeed, it does seem as though everyone is getting married in the Late Period. Where there were usually two couples per book in the Middle Period, there are, in the Late Period, usually three, often four, and sometimes as many as five. But love is nothing to get all wistful about. It isn't like the descent of Venus; it's like an epidemic. There is nothing soppy about it, as there was in the bilge-literature fashion.

In the Middle Period, love and marriage are the concerns of young people exclusively. The older generation is made up of confirmed bachelors, happy widowers, or married people who take marriage for granted. The excitement of love rests with the younger generation, and the novels are primarily concerned with men and women in their twenties.

In the Late Period, there is a new concern for elderly lovers. Beefy Bastable, Lord Tilbury, Albert Peasemarch, and Sir Gregory Parsloe-Parsloe all get married. Even Lord Emsworth is momentarily carried away by "the divine pash," though nothing comes of it. He is, after all, more or less married to his pig.

Wodehouse also marries off his most prominent bachelors such as Oofy Prosser, Freddie Widgeon, Barmy Fotheringay-Phipps, and Pongo Twistleton-Twistleton. In a way, we might even think of Bertie as getting married to Jeeves. In *Thank You, Jeeves*, a Middle Period novel published in 1934, when Bertie insists on practicing the banjolele, Jeeves withdraws his support and aid. In *Jeeves and the Feudal Spirit*, a Late Period novel published twenty years later in 1954, though Jeeves disapproves of Bertie's moustache, he rallies round all the same, and even Bertie is pleasantly surprised at such feudal spirit. The employer-employee relationship of the Middle Period now more resembles a marriage.

Later, the "marriage" is confirmed when Jeeves destroys the eighteen pages he has written about his master for the club book, thus making it impossible for Bertie to get another valet. As he explains,

> "The club book was never intended to be light and titillating reading for the members. Its function is solely to acquaint those who are contemplating taking new posts with the foibles of prospective employers. This being so, there is no need for the record contained in the eighteen pages in which you figure. For I may hope, may I not, sir, that you will allow me to remain permanently in your service?"
>
> "You may indeed, Jeeves."

This may, indeed, be the most romantic passage in the entire Late Period. It has always been the relationship between Jeeves and Bertie that has interested the reader, not the romances that underpin each narrative. (I have found that people, when trying to place the name of a Wooster/Jeeves story, will recall the article of clothing, or whatever, that Jeeves wants Bertie to give up, not the romantic couple(s) in the story.)

Love is still present in the Late Period books, but it is being looked at from new angles, and there is some consideration of divorce. In

Pearls, Girls and Monty Bodkin (1972) for instance, Ivor Llewelyn's divorce at the end is actually a happy closing to the novel. Marriage is still the proper goal for young people in love, and divorce is to be avoided, but it is no longer as clear cut.

Another pattern in the Middle Period is the violence that begins with *Leave it to Psmith*, increases in intensity until *The Code of the Woosters*, and then declines gradually again. The violence can be the harmless destruction of property in anger, such as Aunt Dahlia's smashing the porcelain figure of the Infant Samuel At Prayer, or the Duke of Dunstable's demolition of his nephew's sitting room with a poker; or it might be quite a violent attack on a character—usually someone the reader doesn't like—such as Tubby Vanringham's throttling of Sam Bulpit in *Summer Moonshine* (1937). The worst violence done to a character is the mayhem committed on Roderick Spode in *The Code of the Woosters*: Gussie Fink-Nottle hits him over the head with a painting, then Bertie ties him up, hits him on the head with a vase, and finally puts his cigarette out on Spode's hand.

Such violence is generally skirted in the Late Period, as we can see by comparing the two passages from *Money in the Bank* and *Something Fishy* quoted above. In the former, there is a detailed description of the contact between the tobacco jar and the young man's head and the subsequent results; in the latter, it is carefully avoided. Violence still occurs in the Late Period, but when it is described, it is done without much detail.

The Late Period also sees a sharp increase in references to previous books, some of which are quite obscure and even unnecessary. Any book in a saga is studded with references to past works in the same saga, but in the Late Period, there are far more references to works not contained in the same saga. Characters from earlier books are dug up for just a few lines; Valley Fields, for instance, is mentioned in two non-Valley Fields books as mere passing references. Sometimes, the references are quite obscure indeed, e.g. Isabel Bond's remembrance of a man she knew "who came home on New Year's morning and mistook the coal scuttle for a mad dog and tried to shoot it with a fire tongs. Fellow named Fish." We know from Gally Threepwood's conversation with Lady Julia in *Heavy Weather* that this fellow was Ronnie

Fish's father. The quick reference is the only connection between the two books, and it does nothing to further the plot of the latter book, but it does serve to bring a smile of recognition to the reader's lips. In the Late Period, these kinds of gratuitous references back to earlier works proliferate, especially as time goes on. The final books are chock-full of them.

Some of the references take the form of in-jokes or whimsical fancy. In *Service with a Smile* (1962), Wodehouse gives the address of the millionaire Jimmy Schoonmaker as 1000 Park Ave—Wodehouse's own address in New York in the 1930s. In *Ice in the Bedroom* (1961), Chimp Twist as the detective J. Sheringham Adair offers to employ some of his "best men," including in the list "Meredith [and] Schwed," the names of Wodehouse's agent and editor, respectively. In the short story "Life with Freddie" found in *Plum Pie* (1966), a firm that purchases a large quantity of Donaldson's Dog Joy is Beatle Beatle and Beatle of Liverpool, an obvious reference to the highly popular rock group.

The last reference, however, brings up our final change in patterns between the two mature periods of Wodehouse's writing. The Middle Period takes place roughly between the two World Wars, and the atmosphere in all the books of this period is that of the Roaring Twenties. (With the exception of only a few off-hand references, the Great Depression did not exist in the Wodehouse world.)

Wodehouse scholar R. D. B. French notes, "When Psmith comes to Blandings in *Leave it to Psmith* everything about the book suggests a date before 1914."[5] He does not state why Wodehouse places the story so early, and indeed, this date is really unsupportable. The action is definitely post-World War I. The use of the term "C-3" alone would place it after 1915, but there are other considerations as well. The descriptions of the clothes, the economic climate, and the attitude of the younger female characters all show that this story is set at the time it was written, viz. the early 1920s.

Perhaps what threw French off is the fact that this story doesn't really fit at any time in England. *Leave it to Psmith* marks Wodehouse's first true break from an accurate Edwardian England. Wodehouse was no longer interested in showing life as it actually was, but rather created

5   R. D. B. French, *P. G. Wodehouse* (London: Oliver and Boyd, 1966), 61.

a parallel universe, where things look more or less as in real life, but which is frozen in time.

If the time of the Middle Period may be described as having stood still, however, we may say of the time of the Late Period that it has run amok. We see young men in spats dancing rock 'n' roll and banning the hydrogen bomb, and millionaires complaining of the stock market crash and watching television. Wodehouse has indeed created a parallel universe, but in the Late Period, he draws from any aspect of any period in Britain's post-1917 history to outfit it.

The Late Period was, basically, a time for breaking all the rules, including those that Wodehouse himself had set. We have, then, a Jeeves novel without Bertie (*Ring for Jeeves*), and a Blandings Castle story that takes place entirely on Long Island, New York ("Birth of a Salesman" first published in *This Week*, March 26, 1950). It doesn't always succeed, but it is a rather adventurous spirit that is guiding the way. The theme of the patterns of the Late Period stories may be summed up in Wodehouse's favorite phrase: "Anything Goes."

VI. LANGUAGE

The most striking change one notices in *Full Moon* (1947) is, oddly enough, a much finer distinction than those we have been discussing until now, to wit, a change in Wodehouse's use of imagery. In the Middle Period, Wodehouse would often use a central image throughout a novel, usually one having some connection with the title. The best example is *Heavy Weather* (1933). The main conflict in the book deals with Ronnie Fish's insane jealousy about Sue Brown, his fiancée, which she calls his "making heavy weather." The weather throughout the novel is, indeed, oppressively hot and humid. At the tensest moment in the story, there is a vicious thunderstorm, and, after Ronnie and Sue become reconciled, the air becomes fresh, sweet and cool.

Wodehouse obviously began *Full Moon* with similar intentions toward using a central image. The story opens with the moon "nearly at its full," and we are introduced to the characters by following its rays. The moon waxes slowly over Blandings, as the two pairs of lovers grope toward their mutual unions. The high point comes with Tipton and Veronica walking in the moonlight. The moon is discussed, and they turn in, but Tipton is all a-twitter, as the moonlight "seemed to beckon to him." He goes out again to find solitude on the moonlit terrace, but Lord Emsworth finds him, briefly mentions the moon, and then turns to his favorite topic, his pig. He talks so much at length about his pig that the lovesick and disgusted Tipton wishes "that his companion would trip over a moonbeam and break his neck."

In fact, everything that can possibly be done with the moon is exploited in Chapter Four, and the reader—going on past form—expects it to continue, but, except for one later casual reference back to the moonlight walk, Chapter Four is the last time the moon is mentioned in the book.

If one works out the time sequence in *Full Moon*, he will notice that the moon would indeed be full by the last chapter, but Wodehouse does not point this out. It is obvious that, when sketching out the book, Wodehouse had intended to use the familiar imagery structure, but decided against it when it came to finishing it. It might be argued that since he was interrupted in the writing of the novel, he simply forgot what he originally planned to do when he finally got around to completing it, but I think not. There is no other case in the Late Period of a book with one central image. Wodehouse had abandoned that structure in favor of a multiplicity of images.

He also stopped making his titles serve as double entendres. In the Middle Period, the titles of the books often serve two purposes, sometimes diametrically opposed. (When he used titled chapters, it was often true of those as well.) The best example is *Money for Nothing* (1928), where Mr. Carmody and the Molloys are trying to get capital without honest labor. When the plan falls through, Mr. Carmody, realizing that his initial investment will not pay off, cries: "Money... money... money... and all for nothing."

There are many other examples of this kind of double entendre, usually playing off a popular expression, e.g., *The Small Bachelor* (1927), *Hot Water* (1932), and *Money in the Bank* (1942). In the Late Period, there are titles equally suited to this kind of usage, e.g. *Something Fishy* (1957) and *Ice in the Bedroom* (1961), but the possibilities are never explored.

Leave it to Psmith (1923), also, begins Wodehouse's career in creating new slang expressions. He had used expressions like "C-3" and "oojah-cum-spiff" before, but he begins, in 1923, to start something new, as when Psmith says to Mike Jackson: "let us trickle into yonder tea-shop and drink success to the venture in a cup of the steaming." According to lexicographer and expert on British slang, Eric Partridge, this is the first use of the word "trickle," to mean "to go,"[6] and "steaming," originally a military term for pudding, to mean tea.[7] Other terms, such as "zippy" are first seen in *Leave it to Psmith*, and expressions, such as "pip-pip," are given new meaning. Other new words are added to English and American slang in subsequent books of the Middle Period, e.g. "turpy," "teuf-teuf," "snappers," "buzzer," and many more.

These discoveries and inventions come to an end with the final addition of "oompus-boompus" in *Money in the Bank*. Beginning with *Full Moon*, no new slang words are invented by Wodehouse or his characters.

Several scholars have noted an increase in the ratio of dialogue to narration after *Leave it to Psmith*. For instance, taking *The Coming of Bill* (1919) to represent the Early Period, we see dialogue as 32.5 percent and narration as 67.5 percent of the first ten thousand words of the book. Taking *Heavy Weather* from the Middle Period, the proportion works out to a more conservative 46 percent dialogue, 54 percent narrative. Similarly, there is again an increase of dialogue in the Late Period. In the later books, there are pages upon pages of just dialogue with only a "he said" or "she said" among them. In the Late Period, description and detail are trimmed to the bone. There is no need for them anymore. We have met most of the characters before; we have already seen Blandings Castle or Brinkley Manor, and even if the country house where the action takes place is one we haven't visited, it is enough like the others as to make no difference. Much is lost in such trimming, as some of Wodehouse's grandest style is in his descriptions, but the dialogue is much zippier and more humorous.

The fact is that, like everything else, we can see the narrator moving from Psmithian style to a Bertie zippi-ness. This final observation is the most speculative and touchy, for it is the least empirical, and it is best to discuss it in a section unto itself.

---

6   Eric Partridge, *A Dictionary of Slang and Unconventional English* (London: Routledge & Kegan Paul, 1961), 909.
7   Ibid, 827.

VII. AUNTS AREN'T GENTLEMEN

"Give Bertram Wooster a good, clear story to unfold, and he can narrate it well," says Bertie in *The Code of the Woosters*. His modesty is humorous, for the reader is already enchanted with Bertie's story-telling abilities. The Wooster/Jeeves saga is undoubtedly the most popular in the entire Wodehouse Canon. Evelyn Waugh once said he could not imagine a Wodehouse book without Jeeves, though he was quite aware that there are many of them. After 1945, Wodehouse, too, was quite aware that Bertie Wooster was his most popular character, and, in the Late Period, he wrote more Wooster/Jeeves novels than those of any other saga.

We can, especially after noting all the movements from Psmith to Bertie in the split between the Middle and Late Periods, say that, in a way, Psmith haunts all the books of the Middle Period and Bertie haunts the Late. We might even push this so far as to say that Psmith is the narrator of the third-person novels of the Middle Period, and Bertie, when he isn't telling his own stories, after 1945, is telling all the others. This is, of course, a gross oversimplification and should not be pushed too far, but I think it gives us a clue to—and a feeling for—the subtle, ineffable change on the part of the narrator voice of the third-person books after *Full Moon* (1947).

We see many of Bertie's characteristic phrases popping up in the third-person novels of the Late Period. Let us sample some of these Woosterisms:

As he latch-keyed himself into Peacehaven, one would not be far wrong in saying that there was a song on his lips.

It was one of those avant-garde plays which bring the scent of boiling cabbage across the foot-lights and in which the little man in the bowler hat turns out to be God.

If ever he had seen a fermenting aunt, this fermenting aunt was that fermenting aunt.

Correction. A word as weak and inadequate as "said" should never have been employed when such verbs as "chanted," "carolled," or even "fluted" were at the chronicler's disposal.

There are a host of others as well. It is not pure Bertie Wooster, but it is close; one might say it is the style of a Bertie Wooster who has spent a little more time around Jeeves.

This is not mere speculation and fancy. Wodehouse's last book, *Aunts Aren't Gentlemen* (1974), a Wooster/Jeeves novel, shows us something rather interesting about Wodehouse's time factor. In the opening chapter, Bertie remembers "my American pal, Tipton Plimsoll, with whom I had dinner last night to celebrate his betrothal to Veronica Wedge." In *Galahad at Blandings* (1965), Tipton refers to this same dinner, but in a tone that suggests it was in the more distant past.

We can see, then, that *Aunts Aren't Gentlemen* is meant to take place immediately after the events recorded in *Full Moon*. Therefore, by extrapolation, since all the novels of the Late Period are connected in some way to all the others, we can see that all the third-person novels of the Late Period take place after the last Wooster/Jeeves novel; in fact, after Bertie "has spent a little more time around Jeeves."

Aunts Aren't Gentlemen has a number of other surprising aspects to it. But, by way of examining them, let me first note that it is surprising that the book was written at all. In the Wodehouse Canon, once we have followed a character through his romance, we do not see him in married life (the notable exception being Bingo Little). I have noted earlier that the relationship between Bertie and Jeeves is more like a romance than that of a master and servant, and that the end of *Much Obliged, Jeeves* (1971) is very much like a marriage. It even ends with Bertie quoting to Jeeves, and then making up a colorful phrase of his own, quite a turn in the normal course of events. It is therefore surprising that we are given another book dealing with these two characters. A close examination of this remarkable novel will show us why we are so lucky.

First of all, *Aunts Aren't Gentlemen* is the first Wodehouse book since *A Damsel in Distress* (1919) to have only one pair of lovers, and even they are not the kind the reader feels for. The de-emphasizing of love has been taken a step further. Also, stylistically, *Aunts Aren't Gentlemen* begins where *Much Obliged, Jeeves* leaves off. In the first chapter, Bertie quotes "the poet Ogden Nash" to Jeeves and, indeed, the two characters continue quoting to each other throughout the book. But beyond these minor elements, the novel begins something entirely new and more important.

In the Middle Period, Wodehouse often introduced a mystery early in the novel and let the reader in on it about half-way through. In *Summer Moonshine* (1938), the character of Sam Bulpitt is a very mysterious figure, appearing on a hill during the first tense scene (much like Sherlock Holmes in *Hound of the Baskervilles*), and popping up asking strange questions. Later he is identified, and the mystery is cleared up. This same kind of mystery occurs in other books such as *Big Money* (1931) and *Hot Water* (1932).

Wodehouse drops this very effective device in the Late Period. (A possible exception may be the question of the identity of the man who dropped out of the tontine in *Something Fishy* (1957), but Wodehouse does not play on it in the same way.) In *Aunts Aren't Gentlemen*, this aspect is introduced again, with people popping up all the time asking Bertie, "Has he brought it yet?" It is soon explained to him what they are talking about, and the mystery is solved.

But there is a deeper mystery in the novel, which Bertie sums up as "The Curious Case Of The Cat Which Kept Popping Up When Least Expected." Bertie is trying to get rid of a cat that his Aunt Dahlia has had kidnapped and sent to his place. The first time he sends it back with its kidnapper—the town poacher, Billy Graham—Graham returns with the cat saying it followed him back, and he wants more money to return it again. Bertie questions the poacher's veracity and ends up returning the cat himself. When he arrives home and finds the cat on the premises, he is unable to figure out how it got there.

Even by the end of the novel, the mystery is never solved, but the intelligent reader will see the hand of Jeeves at work. Jeeves had gone to visit his aunt, who lives in the village they are visiting, and he is absent for a great deal of the book. It is this same aunt, whom we never see, who solves the problem of the book by claiming original ownership of the cat, thus letting Bertie off on charges of theft. Jeeves wants Bertie to leave Maiden Eggsford and go to New York, which they eventually do. What better way to get the young master to shift-ho than to keep him festooned with hot cats? Besides, we never learn anything about this aunt of his. Is it not possible that she didn't really own the cat, but that Jeeves had her claim ownership in order to straighten everything out?

Of course, this is all speculation, but the very fact that speculation is possible shows that this is a very different Wooster/Jeeves story. In the past, Bertie would always end up with the full details of Jeeves's machinations; otherwise, the reader would never know what they were. But now, Wodehouse is making us work harder to learn all the facts. He is forcing us to be more intelligent than Bertie; he is, in fact, forcing us to see Jeeves's point of view.

Fanciful speculation is, I think, an ideal way to end this review because that's the nice thing about P. G. Wodehouse: he invites fancy. He has, as Evelyn Waugh said, "made a world for us to live in and delight in"; and even when we are critically studying that world, instead of sitting back and casually reading about it, why shouldn't we live in it and delight in it? It is all part of the great plan of spreading sweetness and light.

From the corner booth, Musso & Frank's Grill
Hollywood, CA
February 14, 2018

The Last Word

CURTIS *and* ELLIOTT *sit at the table. The restaurant is bustling, but not overly noisy. The* WAITER *has just stopped by the table delivering two martinis in the classic Musso & Frank's manner: small martini glasses half-full, with two small carafes containing another 4 or 5 ounces of the clear, delicious liquid sitting in a small pewter bucket of ice. On the table between them lies a thick stack of paper, the proof sheets of their manuscript,* A Plum Assignment.

ELLIOTT. Well, old horse, I think that's it. Put a fork in it; it's done.

CURTIS. Yes, I think so.

ELLIOTT (*lifting his glass*). A toast, then!

CURTIS (*lifting his glass*). To a job well-done!

　　　They clink glasses and sip.

ELLIOTT. Really, though? Do you really think we've got it?

CURTIS. I think so. I think so. But are *you* happy with it? I mean, this was *your* idea after all.

ELLIOTT. Well, you know, I'm still a little disappointed we couldn't put the whole thesis in —

CURTIS. El, we talked about this.

ELLIOTT. I know.

CURTIS. You agreed. Your undergraduate thesis was brilliant. Everyone said so. You were faced with hide-bound and reactionary professors who claimed it couldn't be done. That it shouldn't be done! But you fought the good fight, and you did it! It was, by the account of everyone who has ever read it—even by those who didn't quite make it all the way through—

ELLIOTT. Hey! What?

CURTIS (*hurriedly*). Everyone said it was a remarkable piece of scholarship and far beyond what anyone expected! And yet—

ELLIOTT. I know—

CURTIS. —and yet . . . it *is* an undergraduate thesis! A *long* undergraduate thesis. Too long for the book, laddie.

ELLIOTT. I know. You were right. It's just—

CURTIS. The abridged version is fine. It's great. People will get the point; that's what matters. (ELLIOTT *seems unconvinced.*) And it's much more entertaining!

ELLIOTT. You think?

CURTIS. *So* much more entertaining! A lot better. I mean, *yards* better, to be honest, if you compare the two. Actually, there's no comparison at all—

ELLIOTT. No, I get it! The new version is definitely more entertaining.

CURTIS. That's it. That's all I'm saying. (*They both take a drink. Pause.*) You know what I like? I like how our two styles mesh so well!

ELLIOTT. Oh, they do mesh well!

CURTIS. Very well! We have similar voices, and yet . . . different.

ELLIOTT. Very different! I think I'm more scholarly but you have more . . . style. (*He takes a sip from his drink*). My approach is much more straightforward, more academic. But you're more . . . I don't know . . . more (*he searches for the word*) . . . clever.

CURTIS. Oh, I don't know that I'd say that! No! Clever? Really? I definitely wouldn't say that! (*They both take another drink. Pause.*) Okay, sure, maybe a *little* more clever. And because of the subject matter, we both sound a little Wodehousean. I like that, too.

ELLIOTT. Yes, well mine is self-consciously done. Yours is natural. People noticed the Wodehouse touch in your memoir, and there your subject matter wasn't even Wodehouse.

CURTIS. The supreme trick is to blend serious scholarship with humor, and that is something you make appear deceptively easy.

They toast each other again.

ELLIOTT. Anyway, the fact is that I have spent more time *studying* Wodehouse, but you have read so much more, and it informs your writing with broader understanding. I think that's obvious and it comes through well.

CURTIS. Well, what I think is interesting is how the book has evolved. You saw it more as an historical document: "This is what we wrote about Wodehouse and when we wrote it." But I always thought of it more as a journey. And we take the reader on the journey with us: two friends discovering the joys of Wodehouse together. I mean, there's plenty of scholarship here for even most serious scholar. But the casual Wodehouse reader can enjoy it just as much because they will enjoy seeing how a friendship forms around books. Any bookish person will like this. You know what it reminds me of? *Skye High!* You remember, that book I got you for your birthday a few years ago.

ELLIOTT (*looking into the distance*). Oh yes, of course.

Pause.

CURTIS. You know, the Pearson and Kingsmill book about the two Johnsonian scholars who talk about Boswell and Johnson during a long walking tour in the Hebrides?

ELLIOTT (*busily refilling the glasses from the carafes*). Here, let me freshen you.

CURTIS. You . . . you haven't read it, have you?

ELLIOTT. Well, you know, what with one thing and another . . .

CURTIS. Indeed. Catching up on your Kakfa and Proust?

ELLIOTT. It's just that I was, uh . . . (*his voice trails off.*)

CURTIS. Well. You really should read it.

ELLIOTT. I will.

CURTIS. You'll enjoy it, that's all I'm saying.

ELLIOTT. I'll make it my next read.

    The two friends smile at one another and raise their glasses. Sip.

CURTIS. You still have it, right?

ELLIOTT. Oh yes! (*mutters*) Somewhere . . .

CURTIS. I could send you another.

ELLIOTT. No, no. I still have it, I'm sure. I'll put it on my nightstand as soon as I get home. I promise. I *swear!*

CURTIS. Oh, don't do it on my account. No need for oaths. It's fine. Whatever suits you.

    WAITER *comes by.*

WAITER. Another, gentlemen?

CURTIS. Yes, I think so. Both again?

ELLIOTT. My dear fellow, need you ask?

CURTIS (*to the* WAITER). Yes, please.

    WAITER *departs.*

ELLIOTT. Do you think Wodehouse ever ate here?

CURTIS. Had to have, I should think. Everyone came to Musso's, and he was always a solid trencherman.

ELLIOTT. The only Hollywood restaurant he mentions, though, is The Brown Derby.

CURTIS. Well, it was the most famous in his day.

ELLIOTT. And where is it today? Gone.

CURTIS. With the snows of yesteryear. Chop houses come and go . . . but a good friend, like a good book, endureth.

ELLIOTT *(smiling)*. To the book!

CURTIS. To the book! *(They toast and drain the last of their first martinis as the WAITER silently delivers their second round.)* In fact, to books in general. *(They raise their new martini glasses.)* May they always light our way and quicken our hearts. *(Sip. Sip.)* By the way, did I mention I just started re-reading Lawrence's *Women in Love* and I noticed the damnedest thing—

ELLIOTT *(blanching at Lawrence's name)*. Quite. But maybe we could get back to *our* book for a moment?

CURTIS. Hm? Oh! Oh, certainly!

ELLIOTT. Are you sure you're okay with the title? I like it, but I know you had reservations.

CURTIS. Well, it's just that the whole "Plum" thing is so overdone. *Plum's Peaches. Plum to Peter. Plum Sauce. Yours, Plum. Plum Pie—*

ELLIOTT. Well, that one was his.

CURTIS. Yes, I suppose he had a right to it. I just feel I didn't know him well enough to call him "Plum".

ELLIOTT. How well *did* you know him?

CURTIS. Not at all.

ELLIOTT. Precisely. And millions of others who knew him even less call him "Plum".

CURTIS. But is it right? No, it's fine, El. If I could have come up with anything better, I would have. Any other concerns?

ELLIOTT. Well, even though it's a compilation I feel like we have a responsibility to touch on all aspects of his writing—not the musicals and plays perhaps, but the written works—the novels and short stories.

CURTIS. I think we've done that. Certainly Blandings, Jeeves, Ukridge and Mulliner are well covered between us, and with your thesis—

ELLIOTT. Truncated thesis.

CURTIS. El . . .

ELLIOTT. Sorry. Won't bring it up again.

CURTIS. Anyway, it's pretty comprehensive.

ELLIOTT. Nothing on the golf stories. I feel like they get overlooked all the time. No one, for instance, has ever given a talk on them at the conventions.

CURTIS. Well, what are you doing next year?

ELLIOTT. No thank you! Perhaps you?

CURTIS. I'm up to my eyeballs with this Sherlock Holmes piece I'm working on for the Baker Street Irregulars. Besides, you mention in your thesis how the Oldest Member is derived from W. W. Jacobs. That's something.

ELLIOTT. I suppose . . . You've read Jacobs, haven't you?

CURTIS. Just "The Monkey's Paw."

ELLIOTT. Ah, the standard. You really should try the Nightwatchman stories.

CURTIS. And you should be reading more Washington Irving. Have I ever told you my theory that Wodehouse may have based Blandings Castle on Bracebridge Hall? Fascinating thing—

ELLIOTT (*looking for the* WAITER). Another martini you think?

CURTIS. Two's my limit. Anyway, in 1819 Irving—

ELLIOTT. Well, maybe some champagne then. The occasion certainly calls for it. (ELLIOTT *has succeeded in catching the* WAITER's *eye and he has returned to the table.*) Yes, we'd like a bottle of the Veuve —

CURTIS. Half-bot, I think. I'm about two thirds trolleyed as it is.

ELLIOTT. Don't spoil the ship for a ha'porth of tar, now.

CURTIS. No, El, really.

ELLIOTT (*to the* WAITER, *a little deflated*). Whatever you have in a half-bot that is bubbly, light and appropriate for toasting, please.

    WAITER *departs, not a little deflated himself.*

ELLIOTT. Well, I guess we have everything covered. (*He picks up the manuscript and considers it.*) But it still seems to be missing something.

CURTIS. Elliott, I swear, the abridged version of the thesis is fine. It's great. It's better than great! It's perfect!! Brilliant!! OK? Simply brilliant. No, seriously. It's meticulously researched, richly informative, and executed throughout with all the erudition of the scholar you are, with all the verve and energy of youth, but now tempered by the judicious editing that comes with the wisdom of age. It remains the touchstone of Wodehouse scholarship and loses nothing of its sweep, importance and, dare I say, *fascination*, by being ever so slightly edited for the book. (*Pause*). Don't you agree?

    Pause.

ELLIOTT (*quietly*). I wasn't actually referring to the thesis.

CURTIS. Oh. So, what exactly?

ELLIOTT. I mean, something at the end. Something to wrap it all up—to tie it together.

CURTIS. Like what?

ELLIOTT. Oh, an afterword or something. Something that brings out more of what you were talking about. Two friends talking about books. About Plum!

CURTIS (*wincing*). The Master, *please*!

ELLIOTT. Fine. But do you know what I mean?

CURTIS. You know, now that you mention this afterword idea . . .

ELLIOTT. You've got something?

CURTIS (*wheels turning*). Maybe! Yes! Yes, I just may have!!

ELLIOTT. Well, let's hear it!

CURTIS. Okay, how about this? (*As he speaks, the WAITER arrives with a half bottle of champagne and two champagne flutes, opens the bottle and serves, then puts the bottle on ice and shimmers away.*) We could write a final piece that wraps up everything, as you say, but do it in a way that is stylistically different from everything in the book! It would be sort of elegiac and autumnal. Sad, almost. I mean, we're not the blithe boys we were when we first discovered Wodehouse. We're aging, and the afterword should reflect that! Look at us: We've both been divorced, we have health problems, we're even questioning what we've done with our lives!! We have regrets—*lots* of regrets, really, but through it all we have always turned to Wodehouse for solace. You see? It could be a thoughtful, reflective, mature view of our journey together as scholars and friends as we approach the final dimming of the light. The September of our years. (*Suddenly inspired*) We could call it "As The Curtain Descends"!

ELLIOTT. You know what? Maybe I was wrong. Never mind.

CURTIS. What? You sure?

ELLIOTT. Positive.

CURTIS. I don't know, El. We could write something that would really make them think. Maybe even brush away a silent tear? I mean you were the one who said you wanted to wrap it all up.

> ELLIOTT *picks up his flute of champagne.* CURTIS *joins him. They hold their glasses out to toast.*

ELLIOTT. I know. But really, don't worry about it. (*They toast and sip.*) I'll think of something.

> *The curtain descends.*

ACKNOWLEDGMENTS

In any book of a seriously scholarly bent—or even, as in this case, of a humorously scholarly bent—authors are always keenly aware of the giants' shoulders on which they stand, and *A Plum Assignment* is no different. At every moment of its development, writing, and assembly, there was always an awareness of the contributions of the many—dead or living—who came before and without whose work this volume would have been impossible.

To begin at the beginning: The authors have failed utterly if the reader at this point remains unaware of the importance to this book of Elliott Milstein's University of Toronto undergraduate thesis, "The Growth of Sweetness and Light: The Novels of P. G. Wodehouse." That work would never have come to fruition without the help, generosity, and guidance of Elliott's thesis advisor, Professor James M. Cameron. Professor Cameron guided him through the tangled thickets of researching and composing a thesis, teaching him how to write properly and taking the time to explain the fine points of cricket as well.

If such a thing were enforceable, every book written about P. G. Wodehouse would, by law, include the late Col. Norman Murphy in the Acknowledgments. In the present case, he provided the authors not only with feedback and encouragement, but also with help in researching some items, and offered some kindly editing of articles between their first appearances as live talks and their publications in *Plum Lines*. He was a world class scholar and gentleman and is deeply missed.

Our thanks likewise to Tony Ring, whose scholarship has provided so much information for our pieces. Thanks also to Tony for helping to secure the permission of the Trustees of the Wodehouse Estate for the use of all Wodehouse quotations.

And on that score as well, the authors extend their sincere thanks to Sir Edward Cazalet for his generosity in using his influence to secure that permission and for his kind words of appreciation.

Many of the articles appearing in *A Plum Assignment* were first published in *Plum Lines*, The Wodehouse Society's estimable print organ. Our thanks go to its fine editors Gary Hall and the late Ed Ratcliff. Thanks also to Neil Midkiff, the magazine's behind-the-scenes magician.

Elin Woodger Murphy has been a friend for many years. Whether herding cats on the Executive Committee and the Convention Committee of The Wodehouse Society, or proof-reading for *Plum Lines*, or editing *Wooster Sauce*, or sub-editing many of the articles printed here, Elin has been a leading light in the Wodehouse world for decades. When we asked for a foreword, she jumped to it like a pro. For that, for her kind words and encouragement, and, not least, for some extremely helpful suggestions on the text, we thank her.

Ashley Polasek is deserving of special thanks and gratitude from the authors. A woman with Wodehouse in her bones, she came to do a quick line-edit and months later, was still here, editing, guiding, haranguing, and assembling what might otherwise have been a vanity *jeu d'esprit* and turning it into an actual book. By the end, we came to look upon her not just as an editor, but almost as a co-author, and certainly as a motivating force who always inspired us to be louder and funnier. When the *mot* fell short of the mark, it was Ashley who made it *juste*. Thanks, Ashley.

APPENDIX

A LIST OF THE OPENINGS
TO THE NOVELS OF P. G. WODEHOUSE

The Pothunters (1902)

"Where *have* I seen that face before?" said a voice. Tony Graham looked up from his bag.

Prefect's Uncle (1903)

Marriott walked into the senior day-room, and, finding no one there, hurled his portmanteau down on the table with a bang.

The Gold Bat (1904)

"Outside!"
"Don't be an idiot, man. I bagged it first."
"My dear chap, I've been waiting here a month."

Head of Kay's (1905)

"When we get licked tomorrow by half-a-dozen wickets," said Jimmy Silver, tilting his chair until the back touched the wall, "don't say I didn't warn you."

Love Among the Chickens (1906)

Mr. Jeremy Garnet stood with his back to the empty grate—for the time was summer—watching with a jaundiced eye the removal of his breakfast things.

Love Among the Chickens, Revised Version (1921)

"A Gentleman called to see you when you were out last night, sir," said Mrs. Medley, my landlady, removing the last of my breakfast things.

The White Feather (1907)

"With apologies to the gent opposite," said Clowes, "I must say I don't think much of the team."

Not George Washington (1907)

> I am Margaret Goodwin. A week from today I shall be Mrs.
> James Orlebar Cloyster.

Mike (1909)

> It was a morning in the middle of April, and the Jackson fami-
> lies were consequently breakfasting in comparative silence. The
> cricket season had not begun, and except during the cricket
> season they were in the habit of devoting their powerful minds
> at breakfast almost exclusively to the task of victualing against
> the labors of the day.

A Gentleman of Leisure (1910)

> The main smoking-room of the Strollers' Club had been filling
> for the last half-hour and was now nearly full.

Psmith in the City (1910)

> Considering what a prominent figure Mr. John Bickersdyke
> was to be in Mike Jackson's life, it was only appropriate that he
> should make a dramatic entry into it.

The Prince and Betty (1912)

> A pretty girl in a blue dress came out of the house, and began
> to walk slowly across the terrace to where Elsa Keith sat with
> Martin Rossiter in the shade by the big sycamore.

The Little Nugget (1913)

> If the management of the Hotel Guelph, that London land-
> mark, could have been present at three o'clock one afternoon
> in early January in the sitting-room of the suite which they had
> assigned to Mrs Elmer Ford, late of New York, they might well
> have felt a little aggrieved.

Psmith Journalist (1915)

> The man in the street would not have known it, but a great
> crisis was imminent in New York journalism.

Something Fresh (1915)

> The sunshine of a fair Spring morning fell graciously upon London town. Out in Piccadilly its heartening warmth seemed to infuse into traffic and pedestrians alike a novel jauntiness, so that bus-drivers jested and even the lips of chauffeurs uncurled into not unkindly smiles. Policemen whistled at their posts, clerks on their way to work, beggars approached the task of trying to persuade perfect strangers the burden of their maintenance with that optimistic vim which makes all the difference. It was one of those happy mornings.

Uneasy Money (1916)

> In a day in June, at the hour when London moves abroad in quest of lunch, a young man stood at the entrance of the Bandolero Restaurant looking earnestly up Shaftesbury Avenue—a large young man in excellent condition, with a pleasant, good-humored, brown clean-cut face.

Piccadilly Jim (1917)

> The residence of Mr. Peter Pett, the well-known financier, on Riverside Drive, New York, is one of the leading eyesores of that breezy and expensive boulevard.

The Coming of Bill (1919)

> Mrs. Lora Delane Porter dismissed the hireling who had brought her automobile around from the garage and seated herself at the wheel. It was her habit to refresh her mind and improve her health by a daily drive between the hours of two and four in the afternoon.

A Damsel in Distress (1919)

> Inasmuch as the scene of this story is that historic pile, Belpher Castle, in the county of Hampshire, it would be an agreeable task to open it with a leisurely description of the place, followed by some notes on the history of the Earls of Marshmoreton, who have owned it since the fifteenth century.

Unfortunately, in these days of rush and hurry, a novelist works at a disadvantage. He must leap into the middle of his tale with as little delay as he would employ boarding a moving tram-car. He must get off the mark with the smooth swiftness of a jack-rabbit surprised while lunching. Otherwise people throw him aside and go out to picture palaces.

Jill the Reckless (1920)

Freddie Rooke gazed coldly at the breakfast-table. Through a gleaming eye-glass he inspected the revolting object which Barker, his faithful man, had placed on a plate before him.

Indiscretions of Archie (1921)

"I say, laddie!" said Archie.

The Girl on the Boat (1922)

Through the curtained windows of the furnished flat which Mrs. Horace Hignett had rented for her stay in New York, rays of golden sunlight peeped in like the foremost spies of some advancing army.

The Adventures of Sally (1922)

Sally looked contentedly down the long table. She felt happy at last. Everybody was talking and laughing now, and her party, rallying after an uncertain start, was plainly the success she had hoped it would be.

Leave it to Psmith (1923)

At the open window of the great library of Blandings Castle, drooping like a wet sock, as was his habit when he had nothing to prop his spine against, the Earl of Emsworth, that amiable and bone-headed peer, stood gazing out over his domain.

Bill the Conqueror (1924)

With a sudden sharp snort which, violent though it was, expressed only feebly the disgust and indignation seething within him, Sir George Pyke laid down the current number of Society Spice, and took up the desk-telephone.

Sam the Sudden (1925)

All day long, New York, stewing in the rays of a late August sun, had been growing warmer and warmer, until now, at three o'clock in the afternoon, its inhabitants, with the exception of a little group gathered together on the tenth floor of the Wilmot Building on Upper Broadway, had divided themselves by a sort of natural cleavage into two main bodies—the one crawling about and asking those they met if this was hot enough for them, the other maintaining that what they minded was not so much the heat as the humidity.

The reason for the activity prevailing on the tenth floor of the Wilmot was that a sporting event of the first magnitude was being pulled off there—Spike Murphy, of the John B. Pynsent Export and Import Company, being in the act of contesting the final of the Office Boys' High Kicking Championship against a willowy youth from the Consolidated Eyebrow Tweezer and Nail File Corporation.

The affair was taking place on the premises of the former firm, before a small but select audience consisting of a few stenographers, chewing gum, and some male wage slaves in shirt sleeves, and Mr. John B. Pynsent's nephew, Samuel Shotter, a young man of agreeable features, who was acting as referee.

In addition to being referee, Sam Shotter was also the patron and promoter of the tourney; the man but for whose vision and enterprise a wealth of young talent would have lain undeveloped, thereby jeopardizing America's chances should an event of this kind ever be added to the programme of the Olympic Games.

The Small Bachelor (1927)

The roof of the Sheridan Apartment House, near Washington Square, New York. Let us examine it. There will be stirring happenings on this roof in due season, and it is as well to know the ground.

Money for Nothing (1928)

The picturesque village of Rudge-in-the-Vale dozed in the summer sunshine. Along its narrow High Street the only signs of life visible were a cat stropping its backbone against the Jubilee Watering Trough, some flies doing deep-breathing exercises on the hot window-sills, and a little group of serious thinkers who, propped up against the wall of the Carmody Arms, were waiting for that establishment to open. At no time is there ever much doing in Rudge's main thoroughfare, but the hour at which a stranger, entering it, is least likely to suffer the illusion that he has strayed into Broadway, Piccadilly or the Rue de Rivoli is at two o'clock on a warm afternoon in July.

Summer Lightning (1929)

Blandings Castle slept in the sunshine. Dancing little ripples of heat-mist played across its smooth lawns and stone-flagged terraces. The air was full of the lulling drone of insects. It was that gracious hour of a summer afternoon, midway between luncheon and tea, when Nature seems to un-button its waist-coat and put its feet up.

Big Money (1931)

On an afternoon in May, at the hour when London pauses in its labours to refresh itself with a bite of lunch, there was taking place in the coffee-room of the Drones Club in Dover Street that pleasantest of functions, a reunion of old school friends.

If I Were You (1931)

Through the wide French windows of the drawing-room of Langley End, the country seat of Anthony, fifth Earl of Droitwich, in the county of Worcester, there was much to be seen that was calculated to arrest and please the eye.

Doctor Sally (1932)

> The eighteenth hole at Bingley-on-Sea, that golfers' Mecca on the south coast of England, is one of those freak holes—a very short mashie-shot up a very steep hill off a tee screened from the club-house by a belt of trees.

Hot Water (1932)

> The town of St Rocque stood near the coast of France. The Chateau Blissac stood near the town of St Rocque. J. Wellington Gedge stood near the Chateau Blissac.

Heavy Weather (1933)

> Sunshine pierced the haze that enveloped London. It came down Fleet Street, turned to the right, stopped at the premises of the Mammoth Publishing Company, and, entering through an upper window, beamed pleasantly upon Lord Tilbury, founder and proprietor of that vast factory of popular literature, as he sat reading the batch of weekly papers which his secretary had placed on the desk for his inspection.

Thank You, Jeeves (1934)

> I was a shade perturbed. Nothing to signify, really, but still just a spot concerned.

Right Ho, Jeeves (1934)

> "Jeeves," I said, "may I speak frankly?"
> "Certainly, sir."
> "What I have to say may wound you."
> "Not at all, sir."
> "Well, then—"
> No—wait. Hold the line a minute. I've gone off the rails.

Luck of the Bodkins (1935)

> Into the face of the young man sitting on the terrace of the Hotel Splendide at Cannes there crept a look of furtive shame,

the shifty hangdog look which announces that an Englishman is about to talk French.

Laughing Gas (1936)

I had just begun to write this story, when a literary pal of mine who had had a sticky night out with the P.E.N. Club blew in to borrow bicarbonate of soda, and I thought it would be as well to have him vet what I'd done, in case I might have foozled my tee-shot. Because, except for an occasional anecdote in the Drones smoking-room about Scotsmen, Irishmen, and Jews and even then I generally leave out the point, I've never told a story in my life. And the one thing all the cognoscenti stress is that you must get started right.

Summer Moonshine (1937)

It was a glorious morning of blue and gold, of fleecy clouds and insects droning in the sunshine.

The Code of the Woosters (1938)

I reached out a hand from under the blankets and rang the bell for Jeeves.
"Good evening, Jeeves."
"Good morning, sir."

Uncle Fred in the Springtime (1939)

The door of the Drone's Club swung open, and a young man in form-fitting tweeds came down the steps and started to walk westwards. An observant passer-by, scanning his face, would have fancied that he discerned on it a keen, tense look, like that of an African hunter stalking a hippopotamus. And he would have been right. Pongo Twistleton—for it was he—was on his way to try to touch Horace Pendlebury-Davenport for two hundred pounds.

Quick Service (1940)

In spite of the invigorating scent of coffee which greeted him as he opened the door, it was withdrawn face and dull eye that the willoughy young man with the butter-colored hair and rather prominent Adam's apple entered the breakfast-room of Claines Hall, the Tudor mansion in Sussex recently purchased by Howard Steptoe of Los Angeles. He yielded to no one in his appreciation of coffee, and a couple of cups would un-questionably go down all right, but nothing could alter the fact that on the previous evening he had got engaged to be married to a girl without a bean and was going to London this morning to break the news to his trustee.

Money in the Bank (1942)

Mr. Shoesmith, the well-known solicitor, head of Shoesmith, Shoesmith, Shoesmith, and so on, of Lincoln's Inn Fields, leaned back in his chair and said that he hoped he had made everything clear.

Joy in the Morning (1946)

After the thing was over, when peril had ceased to loom and happy endings had been distributed in heaping handfuls and we were driving home with our hats on the side of our heads, having shaken the dust of Steeple Bumpleigh from our tyres, I confessed to Jeeves that there had been moments when Bertram Wooster, though no weakling, had come very near to despair.

Full Moon (1947)

The refined moon which served Blandings Castle and district was nearly at its full, and the ancestral home of Clarence, ninth earl of Emsworth, had for some hours now been flooded by its silver rays. They shone on turret and battlement; peeped respectfully in upon Lord Emsworth's sister, Lady Hermione Wedge, as she creamed her face in the Blue Room; and stole through the open window of the Red Room next door, where there was something really worth looking at—Veronica Wedge, to wit, Lady Hermione's outstandingly beautiful daughter, who was lying in bed staring at the ceiling and wishing she had some decent jewellery to wear at the forthcoming County Ball. A lovely girl needs, of course, no jewels but her youth and health and charm, but anybody who had wanted to make Veronica understand that would have had to work like a beaver.

Spring Fever (1948)

Spring had come to New York, the eight-fifteen train from Great Neck had come to the Pennsylvania terminus, and G. Ellery Cobbold, that stout economic royalist, had come to his downtown office, all set to prise another wad of currency out of the common people.

Uncle Dynamite (1948)

On the little branch line which starts at Wockley Junction and conveys passengers to Eggmarsh St John, Ashenden Oakshott, Bishop's Ickenham and other small and somnolent hamlets of the south of England the early afternoon train had just begun its leisurely journey.

The Mating Season (1949)

While I would not go so far, perhaps, as to describe the heart as actually leaden, I must confess that on the eve of starting to do my bit of time at Deverill Hall I was definitely short on chirpiness.

The Old Reliable (1951)

The sunshine which is such an agreeable feature of life in and around Hollywood, when the weather is not unusual, blazed down from a sky of turquoise blue on the spacious grounds of what, though that tempestuous Mexican star had ceased for nearly a year to be its owner and it was now property of Mrs. Adela Shannon Cork, was still known locally as the Carmen Flores place. The month was May, the hour noon.

Barmy in Wonderland (1952)

J. G. Anderson took up the telephone. "Give me the desk," he said. They gave him the desk.

Pigs Have Wings (1952)

Beach the butler, wheezing a little after navigating the stairs, for he was not the streamlined young under-footman he had been thirty years ago, entered the library of Blandings Castle, a salver piled with letters in his hand.

Ring for Jeeves (1953)

The waiter, who had slipped out to make a quick telephone call, came back into the coffee-room of the Goose and Gherkin wearing the starry-eyed look of a man who has just learned that he has backed a long-priced winner.

Jeeves and the Feudal Spirit (1954)

As I sat in the bath-tub, soaping a meditative foot and singing, if I remember correctly, "Pale Hands I Loved Beside the Shalimar," it would be deceiving my public to say that I was feeling boomps-a-daisy.

French Leave (1956)

If you search that portion of the state of New York known as Long Island with a sufficiently powerful magnifying glass, you will find, tucked away on the shore of the Great South Bay, the tiny village of Bensonburg. Its air is bracing, its scenery picturesque, its society mixed.

Something Fishy (1957)

The dinner given by J. J. Bunyan at his New York residence on the night of September the tenth, 1929, was attended by eleven guests, most of them fat and all, except Mortimer Bayliss, millionaires.

Cocktail Time (1958)

The train of events leading up to the publication of the novel *Cocktail Time*, a volume which, priced at twelve shillings and sixpence, was destined to create considerably more than twelve and half bobsworth of alarm and despondency in one quarter and another, was set in motion in the smoking-room of the Drones Club in the early afternoon of a Friday in July.

Jeeves in the Offing (1960)

Jeeves placed the eggs and b. on the breakfast table, and Reginald ('Kipper') Herring and I, licking the lips, squared our elbows and got down to it.

Ice in the Bedroom (1961)

Feeding his rabbits in the garden of his residence, The Nook, his humane practice at the start of each new day, Mr. Cornelius, the house agent of Valley Fields, seemed to sense a presence.

Service with a Smile (1962)

The morning sun shone down on Blandings Castle, and the various inmates of the ancestral home of Clarence, ninth earl of Emsworth, their breakfasts digested, were occupying themselves in their various ways. One may as well run through the roster just to keep the record straight.

Stiff Upper Lip, Jeeves (1963)

I marmaladed a slice of toast with something of a flourish, and I don't suppose I have ever come much closer to saying "Tra-la-la" as I did the lathering, for I was feeling in mid-season form this morning.

Frozen Assets (1964)

The Sergeant of Police who sat at his desk in the dingy little Paris police station was calm, stolid and ponderous, giving the impression of being constructed of some form of suet.

Galahad at Blandings (1965)

Of the two young men sharing a cell in one of New York's popular police station Tipton Plimsoll, the tall thin one, was the first to recover, if only gradually, from the effect of the potations which had led to his sojourn in the coop.

Company for Henry (1967)

Fork in hand and crouched over the stove in the kitchen of his large and inconvenient house, Ashby Hall in the county of Sussex, Henry Paradene had begun to scramble eggs in a frying pan.

Do Butlers Burgle Banks? (1968)

Charlie Yost, the Chicago gunman, called on Horace Appleby one morning in June as he chatted with Basher Evans before going off to the Wellingford races.

A Pelican at Blandings (1969)

The summer day was drawing to a close and dusk had fallen on Blandings Castle, shrouding from view the ancient battlements, dulling the silver surface of the lake and causing Lord Emsworth's supreme Berkshire sow Empress of Blandings to leave the open air portion of her sty and withdraw into the covered shed where she did her sleeping.

The Girl in Blue (1970)

The afternoon sun poured into the office of the manager of Guildenstern's Stores, Madison Avenue, New York, but there was no corresponding sunshine in the heart of Homer Pyle, the eminent corporation lawyer, as he sat there.

Much Obliged, Jeeves (1971)

As I slid into my chair at the breakfast table and started to deal with the toothsome eggs and bacon which Jeeves had given of his plenty, I was conscious of a strange exhilaration, if I've got the word right.

Pearls, Girls and Monty Bodkin (1972)

As always when the weather was not unusual the Californian sun shone brightly down on the Superba-Llewellyn motion picture studio at Llewellyn City.

Bachelors Anonymous (1973)

Mr. Ephraim Trout of Trout, Wapshott and Edelstein, one of the many legal firms employed by Ivor Llewellyn, head of the Superba-Llewellyn studio of Llewellyn City, Hollywood, was seeing Mr. Llewellyn off at the Los Angeles airport.

Aunts Aren't Gentlemen (1974)

My attention was drawn to the spots on my chest when I was in my bath, singing, if I remember rightly, the Toreador song from the opera Carmen.

Sunset at Blandings (post.)

Sir James Piper, England's Chancellor of the Exchequer, sat in his London study staring before him with what are usually called unseeing eyes and snorting every now and then like somebody bursting a series of small paper bags. Sherlock Holmes, had he seen him, would have deduced instantly that he was not in a good temper.

ABOUT THE AUTHORS

CURTIS ARMSTRONG was born in Detroit, MI in 1953, the same year P. G. Wodehouse, then a much older man, wrote *Ring for Jeeves*. Anyone who's read *Ring for Jeeves* knows that's not really anything to brag about. In 1964, having made Detroit too hot to hold him, he moved to Geneva, Switzerland (Curtis, I mean, not Wodehouse, who was living in Remsenberg, Long Island at the time), where for the next several years, he bought Wodehouse's new books like clockwork in those Penguin paperbacks, many of them with Ian Carmichael or Dennis Price on the covers. On returning to Detroit in 1967, he met Elliott Milstein, in whose company he continued to read Wodehouse, though in inferior American editions, for years. He was studying at the Academy of Dramatic Arts in Michigan when, on St. Valentine's Day, 1975, Wodehouse died. P. G. Wodehouse was survived by countless devoted readers all over the world, including Curtis Armstrong who, widely regarded as being unfit for respectable employment, became a professional actor, and has been featured in hundreds of productions on stage, film, and television, none of them having anything to do with P. G. Wodehouse.

ELLIOTT MILSTEIN was born on October 15, 1881 in a log cabin in Chillicothe, Ohio, to a gentleman farmer and fishwife. The youngest of fourteen, and having to make his own way in this world, he punched cows in Arizona, jerked soda in Tennessee, prospected in the Mojave Desert, and did a little newspaper work, ultimately getting a job on the *New York World*, editing its "In What Way?" column. Since then, he has written a dozen unproduced plays and screenplays, several unpublished novels and short stories, and a thesis on P. G. Wodehouse which he has been trying to interest people in for over forty years, to which end he joined The Wodehouse Society (TWS) in 1989, became its Vice President in 1993, and President in 1995. He is also a member of the Dutch P. G. Wodehouse Society and the P G Wodehouse Society (UK), whose meetings he occasionally infests. He has, to date, given seven talks at TWS conventions and threatens to continue doing so until someone listens to him. He finally wound up making his fortune selling drugs on the streets of Detroit. He is survived by a wife, four children and 27 grandchildren and is available for weddings and Bar Mitzvahs.

CPSIA information can be obtained
at www.ICGtesting.com
Printed in the USA
LVHW111130130121
676373LV00010B/297